Learn and Do Photography Unit Study

Copyright © 1998 by  alWright! Publishing

For information, email info@KymWright.com or
Kym Wright
PO Box 81124
Conyers, Ga 30013.

Websites:

www.KymWright.com

www.Learn-and-Do.com

www.Living-Life-on-Purpose.com

www.The-Mothers-Heart.com

International Standard Book Number: 978-1-4276-2072-9

Notes:

Table of Contents

Notes:

Table of Contents

Notes:

How to Use

Welcome to Photography!

This Photography course will cover the components of taking good pictures. We will cover topics such as: shadows, lighting, focal points, foreground, background, displaying pictures and more. What this course will not teach is the technical usage of a camera nor developing film.

You can use an instant camera or a more advanced camera for this course. You will need to read through the literature or User's Manual for your particular camera and model, to learn where the parts are located, how to adjust it, using the flash, etc. If your camera is a more advanced 35 mm, and has F-stops and other "fancy" things, you will need to learn to use this also.

Once you have mastered the basic usage of your camera, come join us in learning to take good pictures!

Throughout this book, you will see various symbols near the outside margin of the page. When you see this sign, it means:

☞   Remember this point or here is some information.

📖   Read about or research this topic. Look in library or personal books, instruction manuals, online, in magazines, or wherever the information is available.

✏   Write on this topic. Define the words, make a list, critique.

✏"   Critique or discuss in writing or verbally. This can be with fellow students, the teacher, a photographer or friends.

🚌   Field trip. Go explore, gain experience, venture on an adventure.

📽   Practice Shots. Take photographs using these guidelines, trying these pointers.

💣   Experiment. Follow the instructions or find your own. Experiment and learn about the many aspects of photographpy.

How to Use

Find it on the computer. Visit a website, do a search, join a chat. (Please read the information about "Online" on page 53 concerning online searching.)

Put the information in your notebook. Put everything into the notebook including pictures (before and after), critiques, lists, and written assignments.

❑ Check off the list. Make sure to do each point discussed or listed.

SETTING UP THE NOTEBOOK
For the notebook you will need:
- ❑ 3-ring notebook
- ❑ dividers (if you want to divide the information into sections such as: photographs, lists, experiments, written assignments, etc. Just remember to keep the critiques with the pictures to which they refer.)
- ❑ lined paper for lists, critiques and written assignments
- ❑ colored pens for captions and descriptions of the photographs

❑ PHOTOGRAPHY MATERIALS NEEDED
- ❑ camera
- ❑ flash ability (flash attachment, flash cube, etc.), unnatural light source
- ❑ film, film and more film
- ❑ place to develop film
- ❑ camera store
- ❑ items for a homemade pin-hole camera (❑ shoe box with lid ❑ nail ❑ white paper ❑ cellophane tape ❑ bright light source ❑ magnifying glass ❑ darkened room)
- ❑ flashlight
- ❑ books on: photography, taking pictures, composition, photojournalism, landscape pictures, panoramas, photographing people, and other related topics (see table of contents)
- ❑ white background for silhouettes (see lesson on silhouettes)

Notes:

How to Use

❏   paper screen for silhouettes (see lesson)
❏   animals to photograph (pets, zoo, in the wild)
❏   special effects lenses (see lesson)
❏   transparent colored cellophane paper
❏   photo albums, if desired
❏   picture frames, if desired
❏   make-your-own greeting cards (may be construction paper or fancier)

Outline

I. Camera Parts
  A. Identify
       1. Viewfinder
       2. Wind-on dial or lever
       3. Rewind lever
       4. Exposure counter or frame counter
       5. Lens
       6. Shutter
       7. Aperture
       8. Shutter button
       9. Shutter-speed dial
       10. Aperture control
       11. Focus control
       12. Flash shoe or attachment (sometimes called a hot
             shoe or flash attachment)
  B. Usage

II. Camera Types
  A. Simple cameras
       1. Easy to begin with
       2. Learn the parts
       3. Learn to take good pictures
       4. Advance to more complicated camera
  B. More complicated camera
       1. More features to learn
       2. Control light
       3. Take pictures in more extreme conditions (light or dark)
       4. Special effects

III. Digital Cameras

IV. Lenses

V. Film
  A. Types

Outline

B. How it works
C. Putting in the camera

VI. Components of taking good pictures
A. Focus
B. Camera Positions
C. Rule of Thirds
D. Focal Point

VII. Lighting
A. Shadows
B. Shading
C. Natural and Unnatural Light
D. Clouds and Sunshine
E. Flash Attachments

VIII. Point of View and Angles

IX. Photographing People
A. Composing, Grouping and Staging
B. Portraits
C. Background
D. Movement
E. Focal Point
F. Self-Portraits
G. Silhouettes and Methods
H. Group Pictures, Formal and Informal Settings, Arranging
I. Photographing Children

X. Landscape Pictures
A. Planning
B. Shooting
C. Panorama Pictures

XI. Patterns and Waterfront
A. Shadow and lighting

Outline

    B. Textures
    C. Reflected Light

XII. Metropolitan Areas

XIII. Action Shots

XIV. Photographing animals
    A. Pets
    B. Zoo
    C. In the wild
    D. Stalking Animals

XV. Special Effects
    A. Mirrors
    B. Filters
    C. Binocular
    D. Microscopic

XVI. Displaying Your Pictures

XVII. Using the Skill
    A. Careers
    B. Hobbies
    C. Experience

XVIII. Clubs, Organizations, Contests
    A. On-line Websites
    B. On-line Chat Groups
    C. On-line Resources
    D. Magazines
    E. Associations

XIX. Vocabulary

XX. Book List

Camera Parts

📖 Read a book about cameras and taking pictures. The book, Click! by Gail Gibbons is great for basic introduction to younger (and older) children. Taking Pictures by Nina Leen is also a good introductory book for five to seven year olds. Both books should be available at your local public library. (See Book List.)

☞ No matter how old or new your camera is, it will have these five basic parts:

❑ **A lightproof box**: keeps unwanted light from the film, allowing light in only when taking a picture to help make the picture.

❑ **Film advance:** moves the film forward, after taking a picture, in preparation for the next picture.

❑ **Viewfinder:** the place the photographer looks through to see what will be in the picture

❑ **Lens:** a curved piece of glass that focuses the light rays from the subject to form a picture

❑ **Shutter:** a little door or window behind the lens that allows the light through to form the picture on the film (it "opens" and "shuts" to allow light through)

Instant Camera

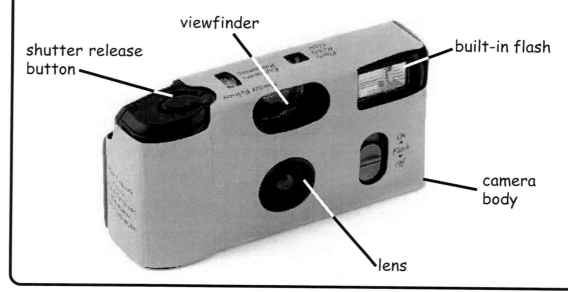

shutter release button

viewfinder

built-in flash

camera body

lens

Camera Parts

Sophisticated
35mm Compact Cameras

flash shoe
(for flash attachment)

shutter release
button

camera
body

lens
(without cap)

aperture control

focusing ring

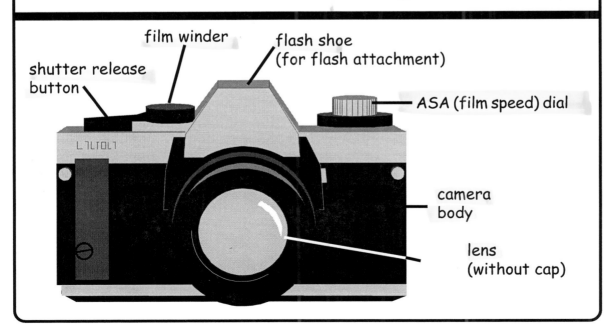

film winder

flash shoe
(for flash attachment)

shutter release
button

ASA (film speed) dial

camera
body

lens
(without cap)

Types of Cameras

There are four main types of cameras:

1.   **Viewfinder**: has a small window showing what the picture will include in it (most "instant" cameras are this type)

2.   **Single-Lens Reflex**: (SLR) uses the same lens for viewing and for taking the picture. The viewfinder lens is the same as the lens that captures the picture.

3. **Twin-Lens Reflex**: has two matched lenses. One to view and frame the picture, the second puts the picture on the film. Usually, the photographer views the subject from above the camera, looking down.

4. **View Camera**: an advanced camera used by professionals. Photographer frames the picture onto a piece of frosted glass at the back of the camera, then replaces the glass with film before taking the picture.

☞ Decide which type camera you have or are using.

✐ Draw a diagram of your camera and label the main parts.

📖 You may want to read about the history of cameras. A Look Inside Cameras is an excellent resource. (See Book List.)

Digital Cameras

Just a few short years ago digital cameras were very expensive curiosities that held much promise, but actually delivered very little. That has greatly changed with the highly competitive digital camera market of today. Prices are falling and quality is increasing. Let's take a look at how a digital camera works compared to a film camera, what to expect if you buy one, and some unique uses.

1. **How it works:** A film camera works by allowing the light from an image being photographed to come through a lens for focus and then through an iris that controls how much light can strike the film for how long. Once you shoot all the pictures on a roll, you submit the film for processing and get back your prints. Some film cameras are fully automatic, and some require manual adjustment. Digital cameras are very similar. The light still comes through a lens and an iris, but the light strikes a sensor array that turns the image into a digital file instead of exposing film. Now this is where the fun begins. Rather than sending your film out for processing and printing, digital cameras download their pictures to a computer and allow you to view or print them instantly. You can also adjust the pictures after you've taken them — to correct, touch up, crop, or distort the image.

Instamatic-type camera

Unique swivel lens camera

Storage of the images on a digital camera varies widely. Some less expensive "instamatic" type cameras have fixed memory inside the camera to store the images with limited capacity. Once you take as many pictures as it will hold, you can't take anymore until you download or delete them. Other digi-

Traditional-type camera

Notes:

Digital Cameras

tal cameras store their images on floppy disks, "Smart Media" cards, flash memory cards, or even miniature harddrives. These allow you to have unlimited picture capacity since you can insert another storage device if your first one fills up before you can download.

2. **What you get:** Digital cameras come with a) the actual camera, b) some form of transfer device to get your pictures into your computer, c) at least one storage device if it uses one, d) software for downloading, organizing, storing, and adjusting your pictures, and e) instruction manuals. There is nothing else to buy when you purchase a digital camera kit. And you won't ever have to pay for film processing again! Less expensive models are available for about $150 . . . high end consumer cameras can cost over $1000.

3. **Unique Uses:** Having the picture on your computer opens up all kinds of opportunities for unique uses. First, you can learn about the types of things you can do in a darkroom since digital images can be adjusted for brightness, contrast, color corrections, cropped, enlarged, and manipulated with an amazing array of effects that can be applied to your picture. (Would you like it to look like an oil painting or a watercolor? Just apply a "filter" and you see it instantly.) My children have hours of fun creating collages of pictures from their field trips or other activities. They also make greeting cards that are personalized with pictures. You can send your pictures to friends and family through e-mail, publish them on a website, burn them on a CDROM disk to create an electronic photo album for the grandparents, or an endless variety of creative uses.

4. **Where to learn about them:** Here are some excellent websites for learning more about digital photography:

Digital Photography Exhibit: *www.bradley.edu/exhibit*
See what others are doing with their digital cameras in this long-running nationwide contest.
PC Photo Forum: *www.pcphotoforum.com*

Digital Cameras

This site provides news, comparisons, and price guides for many models and accessories.

- **Computershopper.com:** *www.computershopper.com*
ZDNet's Computershopper.com lets you comparison-shop by manufacturer, desired features, or price range.

5.	If you don't have a digital camera, plan a field trip to see a demonstration (from a friend, acquaintance, professional or camera shop).

	View or observe the following:
	a)	a digital camera (or several different styles)
	b)	the image in the lens
	c)	taking the pictures
	d)	downloading the images
	e)	the image on the computer screen
	f)	"adjusting" the pictures (see the options under #3 on previous page)
	g)	printing the images on paper (special photography paper or plain white paper)

Lenses

☞ Three of the most basic types of lenses are:
- ❑ **Wide-Angle Lens**: includes a wide view in the picture of what is in front of the camera. Good for taking scenic photos.
- ❑ **Telephoto Lens**: similar to a telescope, it focuses on objects far away, allowing the photographer distance from the subject.
- ❑ **Macro Lens**: similar to a microscope, allowing the photographer to get extremely close to the subject and still capture a focused picture.

📖 Read about lenses.

📖 Read about focusing and autofocusing.

📖 Read about the diaphragm, its role in focusing in different lighting conditions.

📖 Read about shutter adjustments for focusing.

✏ Write down the type of lens(es) your camera has.

✏ Make a list of the types of lenses you would like to try.

📖 Read about the special lenses you listed and those below.

✏ Write a short definition of each of the lenses.

🚌 Field Trip: go to a camera store and look at cameras with the various lens types you listed above, and those below. Look through the viewfinders to see the difference. There are a variety of each of these lenses. View as many of them as possible. Take your list of lenses and their definitions with you when you go to the camera store.
- ❑ Wide-angle lens(es)
- ❑ Telephoto lens
- ❑ Zoom lens
- ❑ Endoscope
- ❑ Automatic focus lens
- ❑ Fish-eye lens
- ❑ Mirror lens
- ❑ Macro lens
- ❑ Perspective-correction lens
- ❑ Colored (gel) filters

📁 Put the list in your notebook.

Film

✎ Write a definition for film.

📖 Read about film.

✎ Make a list of the different types of film.

🚌 Field Trip: Visit a store that carries film and look at each type of film carried.

✎ Make a list of the variety of film carried by the store.

📂 Put the list in your notebook.

✎ How does film work? Write a paragraph explaining.

📖 Read about film speed.

✎ Define film speed and explain how it works.

📖 Read about putting film in various types of cameras. Look at your instruction booklet for directions for your specific model. Learn how to put film in your camera, and others, if available.

📖 Read about developing film.

✎ Define the following words:
- ❑ Negatives
- ❑ Prints
- ❑ Enlarger
- ❑ Exposure
- ❑ Darkroom
- ❑ Enlargements
- ❑ Macro lens

☞ One of the most important things to remember about film, is

not exposing film to light.

☞ Like a stencil, the negative of a picture blocks the light from printing on certain portions of the film paper, and letting light through the pale portions. What is printed becomes the photograph.

35mm film canister

35mm film

110 film (instant cameras)

Lens & Film

Notes:

☞ Simplifying the process, light that bounces off the image and passes through the lens. The light then goes through the opening in the camera, known as the aperture. With instant and compact cameras, this hole has a fixed amount it opens. In more advanced (SLR) cameras the hole (aperture) can be adjusted by the photographer. Measured in *f-numbers* or *f-stops*, these increments change how much of the image is in focus in the photograph. Shutter speed is how long the shutter is left open. When the shutter button is pressed, the shutter opens to allow light in. The light projects onto the film and forms an image. With SLR cameras, the photographer has greater control over the amount of light reaching the film (exposure), so he has more control over the final picture.

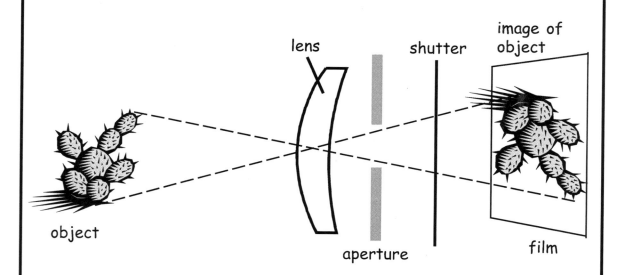

☞ Pressing the shutter button opens a hole to let light in. This light is recorded or imprinted on the film, making an "exposure." When processed, this imprint or exposure becomes a photograph.

© alWright! Publishing

Lens & Film

💣 Experiment: Make a pinhole camera

☞ Materials needed:
- ❑ large shoe box with lid
- ❑ nail
- ❑ white paper
- ❑ tape
- ❑ bright light source
- ❑ magnifying glass
- ❑ darkened room

- ❑ With the nail, poke a hole in one end of the shoe box.
- ❑ Tape the piece of white paper to the inside wall of the box at the opposite end from the hole.
- ❑ Cut a flap in the lid.
- ❑ Tape lid to box around edges.
- ❑ Put a well-lit object in front of the small hole.
- ❑ Turn off overhead lights; make room dark.

End View

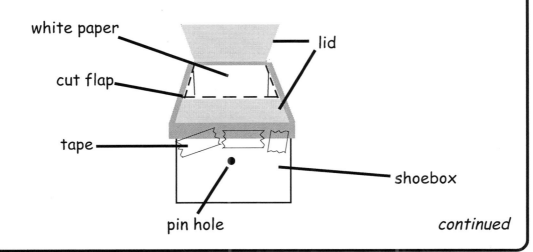

white paper
lid
cut flap
tape
shoebox
pin hole

continued

Lens & Film

Overhead View

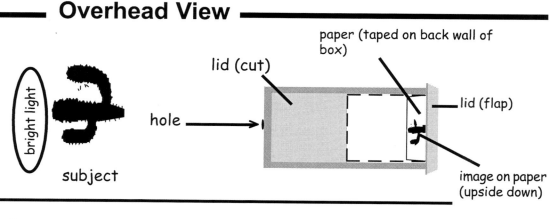

bright light

subject

hole

lid (cut)

paper (taped on back wall of box)

lid (flap)

image on paper (upside down)

✎ Answer these questions, either verbally or in writing.
- ❑ Can you see an image on the white paper at the back of the box?
- ❑ Is the image clear or blurry?
- ❑ Is the image right side up? or upside down?
- ❑ Now try light from different angles: sides, back, above, front, a little to the side, etc.).
- ❑ Does the angle of the light make any difference on the brightness or clarity of the image?
- ❑ Use a magnifying glass in front of the pin hole, much like a lens.
- ❑ Does that make the image more clear? more blurry? brighter?

☞ The camera is similar to the eye, the iris (colored portion of the eye) and the pupil (central black portion of the eye). When you are in very bright light the pupil is small, perhaps just a pinpoint. On a cloudy day the pupil is opened larger. And on a dark, stormy day or at night, the pupil is opened the largest. The shutter and aperture (openings in the camera) work the same way.

💣 To view the action of the pupil, try this experiment. Work in pairs.
- ❑ Observe each other's pupil size in normal daylight.
- ❑ Observe each other's pupil size indoors.
- ❑ Observe each other's pupil size in a darkened room.
- ❑ Using a flashlight, observe each other's eyes while in a darkened room, then shine the flashlight in the eye. You will need to look quickly to observe the immediate change.

✎ Write a paragraph telling what happened and why.

Composition

Kodak's Top Ten Techniques for taking pictures:
1. Keep Your Camera Ready
2. Get Close
3. Keep People Busy
4. Use A Simple Background
5. Place The Subject Off-Center
6. Include Foreground In Scenics
7. Look For Good Lighting
8. Hold Your Camera Steady
9. Use Your Flash
10. Choose The Right Film

Go to this website for more information, answers to "Frequently Asked Questions," "Guide to Better Pictures" and more.
http://www.kodak.com/US/en/nav/takingPics.shtml

Read about focusing the camera.

When taking pictures, use the right hand to hold the camera and to press the shutter button. Focus (if necessary) with the left.

Camera Views

There are basically two ways to hold the camera at a straight angle. The first is called the "landscape" position. The camera bottom is held horizontal to the ground. The picture comes out in a rectangular shape like the one on the right.

camera held at this angle   landscape

The second position is called "portrait" and is accomplished by holding the camera bottom perpendicular (at a right angle) to the ground.

Composition

The picture comes out in a rectangular shape like the one below.

camera held at this angle   portrait

☞ For the portrait view, support camera weight with right hand, while pressing the shutter button with the right thumb. If necessary, focus with the left. (Camera is facing to the right side of your body.)

☞ Portrait position looks best for photographs of people, because both are longer than they are wide, so the dimensions work well together.

☞ Learn to control camera movement: **keep it still!**

☞ Here are some important points to remember when taking pictures:
  ☑ Hold camera with both hands
  ☑ You might need to hold your breath while pushing the shutter button

🎥 Practice Shots #1: with an *unloaded* camera (no film in it), practice "taking pictures" in the portrait and landscape views. Practice holding the camera steady and pushing the button - without moving the camera.

🎥 Practice Shots #2: with film, take a blurry picture and one that is focused. (Blurry shots are made when the camera moves or the subject moves.) Put in your notebook to remind yourself *not* to take blurry pictures! Label.

🎥 Practice Shots #3: with film, take two pictures of the same subject and from the same position and angle - one picture in landscape, the other in portrait. Put in your notebook and label.

Composition

✎ Define: rule of thirds, focal point, foreground, frame, framing, immovable focal point

☞ **Rule of Thirds**: a basic rule of artistic composition that can be used to enhance your photographs. Mentally cut the picture you see out the viewfinder into thirds, with two equally-spaced horizontal lines and two equally-spaced vertical lines. Divide your picture into these thirds, and place your focal point or key objects in the picture on the points where the horizontal and vertical lines bisect (meet). Artistically, this is more pleasing to look at than the focal point being in the center.

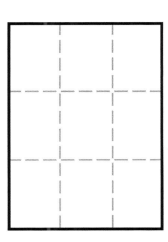

☞ The Rule of Thirds works especially well in photographs of landscapes and horizons. Place the horizon on one of the "thirds." Try to avoid letting the horizon divide a picture in two, or being in the center horizontally.

☞ **Focal point**: Center the subject vertically & horizontally (at first). Expand your ability to have a focal point a bit off-center, but still focal.

☞ Foreground: notice in professional photographs, many times there are things in the foreground that draw the eye in – a tree, branch, bush, building, fence, archway, etc. – framing the shot, but not in the way of the focal point.

📖 Look at pictures with things in the foreground framing the focal point.

☞ When planning a picture, decide what the focal point will be, and the foreground *or* the background. Look for various angles from which to shoot the same subject.

Composition

Notes:

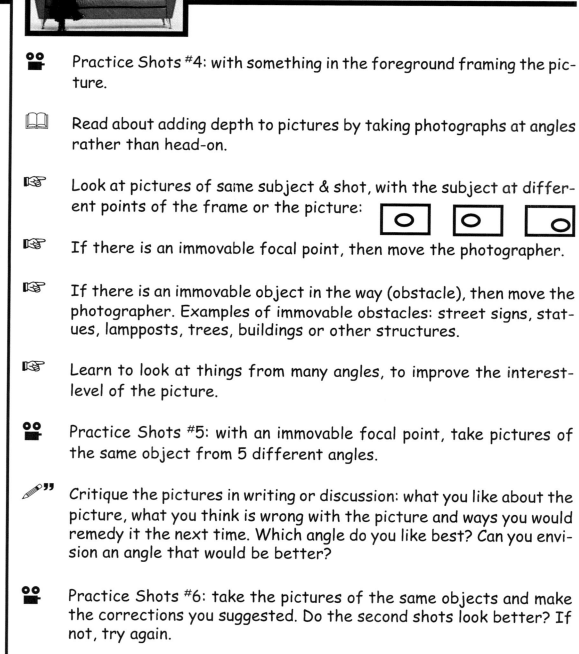

🎥 Practice Shots #4: with something in the foreground framing the picture.

📖 Read about adding depth to pictures by taking photographs at angles rather than head-on.

☞ Look at pictures of same subject & shot, with the subject at different points of the frame or the picture:

☞ If there is an immovable focal point, then move the photographer.

☞ If there is an immovable object in the way (obstacle), then move the photographer. Examples of immovable obstacles: street signs, statues, lampposts, trees, buildings or other structures.

☞ Learn to look at things from many angles, to improve the interest-level of the picture.

🎥 Practice Shots #5: with an immovable focal point, take pictures of the same object from 5 different angles.

✐" Critique the pictures in writing or discussion: what you like about the picture, what you think is wrong with the picture and ways you would remedy it the next time. Which angle do you like best? Can you envision an angle that would be better?

🎥 Practice Shots #6: take the pictures of the same objects and make the corrections you suggested. Do the second shots look better? If not, try again.

📁 Put both sets of pictures - the before and after - in your notebook, along with the critique or a summary.

Lighting

☞   The importance of good lighting can not be stressed enough. It is the most important part of picture-taking.

☞   There are four main sources of light:
- ❏ Sunlight
- ❏ Flash
- ❏ Spotlight
- ❏ Indoor lighting

📖   Read about lighting in photography. *(OTHER SOURCES)*

✏   Define the following words or concepts: artificial lighting, available light, background light, back lighting, bounce lighting, existing light, front lighting, natural light, side lighting and top lighting.

✏   Make a list of the ways to remedy each of these situations:
- ❏ Shadows in the picture:
  - ❏ of buildings
  - ❏ of subject
  - ❏ of photographer
- ❏ Shading
- ❏ Taking pictures of people outdoors on a sunny day
- ❏ Taking pictures outside on a cloudy day

📖   Read about how to work with the following, if you have the equipment and want to use it:
- ❏ Controlling the light with the camera (aperture)
- ❏ Using a light meter

💻   Visit the website: http://www.azuswebworks.com/photography/index.html

☞   A flash fills in if the light is at a back angle or the subject is not illuminated well. Also, if there is plenty of light, but the subject has shadows on the side facing the camera, a flash will reduce the shadowing.

Lighting

📖   Read about how to use flash attachments, flashbar, flashcube, a flash unit, flipflash, hot shoe and anything else related to flash attachments and cameras. Define each of these, or identify them in books.

📖   Read the instruction booklet on the flash system for your particular model.

📖   Read about the cautions of using flashes around window panes, mirrors and other reflective objects.

✏️   Define pink-eye or red-eye as related to taking pictures with flash systems.

📖   Read about the causes and cures of pink-eye or red-eye in photographs.

📖   To reduce chance of "red-eye" pictures, or photos of people with red irises, use a flash extender or flash attachment. These raise the flash above the camera.

✏️   Make a list of the points to remember when using a flash system.

🎥   Practice Shots #1: take pictures outside with flash and outside without flash. Take pictures inside with flash and inside without flash.

✏️   Critique the flash pictures in writing: what you like about the picture, what you think is wrong with the picture and ways you would remedy it the next time. Check for red-eyes, reflected light and any other errors you can see. Review your list of points to remember using a flash system. Did you forget to employ any of the points?

🎥   Practice Shots #2: take the same flash photographs and make the corrections you suggested. Do the second shots look better? If not, try again.

📁   Put both sets of pictures - the before and after - in your notebook, along with the critique.

Notes:

Point of View

✎ Define these words and concepts as related to photography: viewpoint, position, angle, camera angle, center of interest, infinity, perspective, and picture area.

☞ Taking a picture from above a subject makes them look smaller and weaker. Taking a picture from below, while crouching, makes the subject look larger and more powerful. However, shooting pictures of older people from below will result in a more aged appearance because the extra skin under the chin and all the face shadows show up more. Taking pictures from above is a more kind view for older people.

📖 Read about good camera angles and photographer positions for a variety of different viewpoints:
- ❑ Standing
- ❑ Sitting
- ❑ Crouching
- ❑ Kneeling
- ❑ Resting camera on chair back or table
- ❑ Laying on floor
- ❑ Standing above the subject (on chair, table, fence, etc.)
- ❑ Leaning camera on wall, fence, table, desk, etc.

☞ Most often, hold camera horizontal to ground, so picture comes out straight and in the landscape viewpoint.

📹 Practice Shots #1: take pictures of the same subject from the various positions listed above. If you can think of more positions, list them and take pictures from those, also.

✎ Critique the pictures in writing: what you like about the picture, what you think is wrong with the picture and ways you would remedy it the next time. Are the angles good? Which angles worked well, and which did not turn out well? Were any of the positions hard to get into? How can you remedy it? (Carry a stool to get in lower positions, using a tripod, etc.)

Point of View

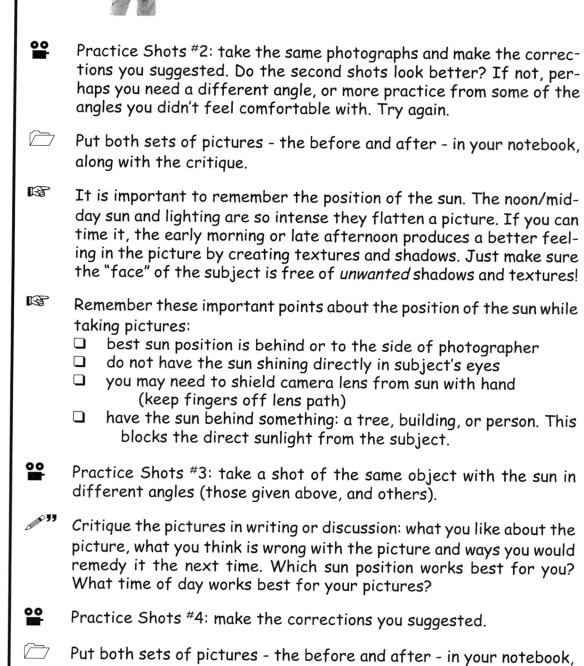

Notes:

Practice Shots #2: take the same photographs and make the corrections you suggested. Do the second shots look better? If not, perhaps you need a different angle, or more practice from some of the angles you didn't feel comfortable with. Try again.

Put both sets of pictures - the before and after - in your notebook, along with the critique.

It is important to remember the position of the sun. The noon/midday sun and lighting are so intense they flatten a picture. If you can time it, the early morning or late afternoon produces a better feeling in the picture by creating textures and shadows. Just make sure the "face" of the subject is free of *unwanted* shadows and textures!

Remember these important points about the position of the sun while taking pictures:
- ❑ best sun position is behind or to the side of photographer
- ❑ do not have the sun shining directly in subject's eyes
- ❑ you may need to shield camera lens from sun with hand (keep fingers off lens path)
- ❑ have the sun behind something: a tree, building, or person. This blocks the direct sunlight from the subject.

Practice Shots #3: take a shot of the same object with the sun in different angles (those given above, and others).

Critique the pictures in writing or discussion: what you like about the picture, what you think is wrong with the picture and ways you would remedy it the next time. Which sun position works best for you? What time of day works best for your pictures?

Practice Shots #4: make the corrections you suggested.

Put both sets of pictures - the before and after - in your notebook, along with the critique or a summary.

People

📖   Read about composing, grouping and staging people for pictures.

☞   Remember the components of good pictures:
- ❏   Shadow
- ❏   Light
- ❏   Focal point
- ❏   Foreground

☞   Remember to look at the background:
- ❏   Color of background in combination with focal point
- ❏   Cluttered or "busy" background? Need to change to a better setting?
- ❏   Moving background?

☞   Remember to look at the middle area between the background and foreground.

✏   After reading and researching, make a list of things to remember when photographing people.

☞   When photographing people remember to:
- ❏   Always ask permission before taking a picture
- ❏   Preset camera - *be ready* – time effectiveness (lighting, focus, etc.)
- ❏   Quick take - take the picture quickly
- ❏   Focal point slightly off-centre (Rule of Thirds)
- ❏   Distance from camera to subject (not too far, nor too close)

🎥   Practice Shots #1: practice presetting the camera and taking pictures quickly. Look for focus, content, lighting, etc.

🎥   Practice Shots #2: with a normal lens, take pictures of the subject very close to the camera (close-up), 3 yards away, and very far away.

People

✏️ Critique the pictures in writing: what you like about the picture, what you think is wrong with the picture and ways you would remedy it the next time. Do you see your quick-pics getting better? More focussed? Better angle and lighting? Capturing the right feeling? Do you like close-up shots? What would make them better? Which position appeals to you the most: close-up, normal distance or far away? Can you think of ways to make your pictures better? Try, try again.

📖 Read about taking pictues of people that don't include their whole body (usually refered to as cutting off body parts).

☞ When you cannot or do not want to include the whole person in a picture, there are some important items to remember about cutting off body parts:
- ❑ never, never, *never* cut off the head
- ❑ cut off above knees rather than below
- ❑ never cut off at a joint, but above it

✏️" In writing or discussion, explain why you think the above rules apply.

📽️ Practice Shots #3: take pictures of people, and cut off different body parts. For this exercise, go ahead and cut off the head, below the knees, before a joint (perhaps a hand).

✏️" Describe how the pictures look. Use good adjectives (descriptive words): complete, incomplete, disabled, chopped, whole, etc.

📖 Read about where the subject should look while having their picture taken. There are different views for different settings.

☞ For balance, most photographers have the subject look directly into the camera or slightly past the camera.

People

Practice Shots #4: take three separate pictures. Have subject look
- ❏ directly into the camera
- ❏ slightly past the camera
- ❏ at a 90° angle from the camera

In writing or discussion, tell how you like each view. Which one draws you into the picture? Rivets you to the picture? Makes you feel an outsider? Gives you a comfortable feeling?

Read about posing the subject: positions, background, foreground, etc.

Remember to try for natural poses:
- ❏ leaning
- ❏ sitting
- ❏ sun to the side (not in their eyes, nor in yours)
- ❏ next to someone or something
- ❏ holding something
- ❏ doing something

Practice Shots #5: just to get used to these ideas, photograph people in some of these settings.

Critique if you would like.

Put all pictures and critiques in your notebook.

Remember to always ask permission to photograph.

Portraits

Notes:

☞ Taking Portraits can be fun. However, you are not just snapping a picture of a person, but letting the photograph say something about the person - their personality, career, hobbies, view of the world and so on. Most importantly, the portrait should look natural.

☞ Make sure nothing in the background looks like it is coming out of the subject's head (lamppost, tree, stick, etc.).

☞ Background: Usually you want to choose an uncluttered background. However, if the person is moving (perhaps a child), take the picture against a strong background - one with an interesting pattern or background. If they move out of position (still in the photo), the background will help it still come out as a good picture.

☞ Focusing the lens on the subject's eyes makes for a nice picture. That is the part of the face to keep in focus.

☞ Ask subject to make a movement. That relaxes the person and makes the photo look more natural and realistic. Take the picture just as they move. This takes practice not to get a blurred picture.

☞ Take many shots so you can choose the best.

☞ Take portraits from several vantage points, viewpoints or angles.

☞ Take with different lighting angles: front, back, side, above.

📽 Practice Shots #1: take portrait photographs using the hints above.

✏ Critique the portrait pictures in writing or discussion: what you like about the picture, what you think is wrong with the picture and ways you would remedy it the next time. Have you captured the person's

Self-Portraits

Notes:

personality or hobbies in the picture? Could you?

Practice Shots #2: take the same portrait photographs and make the corrections you suggested.

Put both sets of pictures - the before and after - in your notebook, along with the critique. Do the second shots look better?

Self-portraits are not as easy as turning the camera around and shooting! Usually a blurred picture results. But, try taking a picture of your reflection. Perhaps a reflection in a metal door, a mirror or another shiny object. *Shoot from the hip*, by keeping the camera at your hip, then you avoid the camera appearing at your face in the picture. Or you can try a delayed action device or timer - these allow you to set a timer for usually 8 seconds after the button is pushed - thereby allowing you to push and run get into place.

Practice Shots #3: take some self-portraits. Be creative in your methods for obtaining pictures of yourself.

Critique the self-portrait pictures in writing or discussion: what you like about the picture, what you think is wrong with the picture and ways you would remedy it the next time. Have you captured your "true" self? Does the picture look like you? Will it give others a feeling of who you are? Is it frame-worthy? What can you do to make it better?

Practice Shots #4: take the same self-portrait photographs and make the corrections you suggested.

Put both sets of pictures - the before and after - in your notebook, along with the critique. Do the second shots look better?

Silhouettes

✏️ Define silhouettes.

☞ Basically, a silhouette is a dark shape on a light background.

📖 Read about making silhouette photographs.

There are two basic methods for making photographic silhouettes.

☞ Method 1: Put darkly-clad subject in front of a white background. Point two spotlights on the white background, one light from each side (lights should not be focused on subject). Take picture.

☞ Method 2: Put subject behind a paper screen (butcher paper, tracing paper, or other thin white paper).
   ❑ Point spotlight from behind subject, onto screen, forming a silhouette of the subject on the screen.
   ❑ Take picture of image on screen.

🎥 Practice Shots #1:
   ❑ Using Method 1, take photograph of a completely darkened silhouetted subject.
   ❑ Using Method 1, take photograph of a somewhat darkened silhouette (can see a touch of reflected light in eyes, on clothes).
   ❑ Using Method 2, take portrait pictures.

✏️” Critique the silhouette pictures in writing or discussion: what you like about the picture, what you think is wrong with the picture and ways you would remedy it. Which method do you prefer?

🎥 Practice Shots #2: take the same silhouette photographs and make the corrections you suggested.

🗀 Put both sets of pictures - the before and after - in your notebook, along with the critique. Do the second shots look better? If not, try again!

Group Pictures

☞ When taking group pictures, the subjects need to "feel" or appear related in some way. Not looking in different directions, but focused on each other, the camera, or looking in the same direction. Touching or putting an arm around others helps the picture look natural.

☞ With informal situations, the faces are not necessarily the focal point, and might be *facing away* from the camera.

☞ For more formal settings or photographs, group according to height – tallest in back, some sitting. Make sure you can see their faces and they are all looking at the camera or at the same focal point.

You can arrange a group of people around one chair. The most important person should sit in the chair, with some of the people standing behind, others sitting on the arms or kneeling beside, and more people sitting in front of the chair. Arrange to please the eye. Tallest in back, shortest in front, like a diamond:

📷 Practice Shots #1: Take some group pictures. Think through the positioning and getting the subjects related in some way. Take several pictures of the same group in different poses.

📷 Practice Shots #2: Some photographers have the group look at a focal point a bit off to the side of the camera, rather than directly into the camera. Experiment with this and see if it pleases your eye.

Photographing Children

📖 Look at group pictures - yours and other photographers' photos.

✏️ Critique the pictures – write a few sentences telling what you feel is right and wrong with the grouping. Then write the ways you would correct it. Try to include copies of the pictures with your sentences.

🎥 Practice Shots #3: take the same group photographs and make the corrections you suggested.

🗀 Put both sets of pictures - the before and after - in your notebook, along with the critique. Do the second shots look better? If not, try again.

☞ When taking pictures of children, it is best for the photographer and camera to be on their level or below their level. If taken from above, the child is looking up at an unnatural angle and looks smaller and weaker. (Work with the child's energy level and interests. If child is tired or crying, the picture will not look as good. Also, if child loves a certain toy, include that in the shot.)

🎥 Practice Shots #4: take pictures of children from different angles: on their level, from above, and below their eye level.

✏️" Critique the pictures in writing or discussion: what you like about the picture, what you think is wrong with the picture and ways you would remedy it the next time.

🎥 Practice Shots #5: try taking pictures of children and make the corrections you suggested. Do the second shots look better? If not, try again.

🗀 Put both sets of pictures - the before and after - in your notebook, along with the critique.

Landscape

☞ Landscape photographs account for the majority of pictures taken. Many times we expect the camera to capture our feelings about the view, "Magnificent!" "Breathtaking!" rather than what we are focusing on with the viewfinder. When taking pictures outside and especially of landscapes, the most important aspect to remember is to **plan the picture.** Don't just "snap" whatever you see.

☞ The noon/midday sun and lighting are so intense they flatten a picture. If you can time it, the early morning or late afternoon lighting produces a better feeling in the picture, by creating textures and shadows. Just make sure the "face" of the subject is free of *unwanted* shadows and textures!

☞ When planning the picture, take the time to look at these points:
- ❑ Lighting
- ❑ Framing or foreground (to fill empty space)
- ❑ Focal point (remember the Rule of Thirds)
- ❑ Points of interest
- ❑ Distance (not too far away, while still creating depth)
- ❑ Moving objects

📖 Look at pictures of landscapes.

☞ Many times good quality landscape photographs will include a road or railway leading into the picture, especially leading towards the focal point. There might be a person in the foreground, a tree or perhaps just a branch in front of the focal point. This helps in creating depth and distance in your picture, rather than having it flat with everything at the same distance from the camera lens.

📽 Practice Shots #1: find a beautiful landscape scene and plan several different angles from which to shoot. Take the pictures.

✏ Critique the landscape pictures in writing: what you like about the picture, what you think is wrong with the picture and ways you would remedy it the next time. Are you pleased with the picture? Did you capture the feeling you desired? Did you plan it well? Does it show?

Panorama

📽 Practice Shots #2: take pictures of the same landscape and make the corrections you suggested. Do the second shots look better? If not, try again.

📂 Put both sets of pictures - the before and after - in your notebook, along with the critique.

📖 Read about panorama pictures.

💻 Visit websites, or look at books on taking panorama pictures.

☞ A Panorama picture is one that captures a horizontal field of view wider than normal pictures. To take a panorama picture without a wide-angle lens, you will need to take several pictures of the same scene, moving from one side to the next. The first picture will cover one side of the scene (for example, the left), the second shot will cover the middle portion, and the last picture will cover the other side (the right). Remember to overlap the pictures a little bit each time, so you will have a point of reference to connect them. After processing, the pictures can be put side-by-side to show a panoramic view of the landscape.

Picture #1   Picture #2   Picture #3

Three separate pictures to capture the same panoramic view of a canyon scene.

Panorama

Practice Shots #3: take pictures of the countryside in a panorama style. After processing, put the pictures side-by-side to show a panoramic view of the landscape.

Critique the pictures in writing or discussion: what you like about the picture, what you think is wrong with the picture and ways you would remedy it the next time. Did you overlap the pictures enough to get a good flow? Would taking four pictures instead of three help the picture?

Practice Shots #4: take pictures of the same landscape and make the corrections you suggested.

Put both sets of pictures - the before and after - in your notebook, along with the critique.

Patterns & Waterfront

📖 Read about shadow and light, positioning the sun to get the best shadows, sand shadows, texture pictures and related topics.

☞ Taking Pattern pictures is easy and the end results are usually pleasing to the eye. There are patterns everywhere you look and often the symmetry of the subject makes for an interesting picture. Patterns can be found in both man-made objects (streets, buildings, stairs etc.) or in nature (trees, leaves, fields, etc.).

📹 Take some pattern pictures - no people, pets or landscapes - just the pattern. Shadows on sand ridges, on the bark of a tree, in rocks on a hill. Observe nature around you, plan the picture and take it.

✏" Critique, plan and 📹 (Practice Shots #2) snap again.

📂 Put both sets of pictures - the before and after - in your notebook, along with the critique.

📖 Read about taking pictures near waterfronts and how to take pictures when there is reflected light.

☞ When taking pictures at waterfronts and when working with reflected light, here are some suggestions on how to remedy specific problems:
- ❑ For bright light, take close-ups or move closer to the focal point.
- ❑ For pictures of the horizon, remember the Rule of Thirds and place the horizon off the horizontal center - usually having it in the bottom third is best.
- ❑ Stick with low-angle views.
- ❑ When taking water shots, keep the camera at a 45° angle from surface of water. This will help to avoid reflections (of you and the camera). Waves and water movement need a faster shutter speed.
- ❑ It is preferable to take pictures at the beach or waterfront on a cloudy day with not so bright sunshine.

📹 Practice Shots #3: Waterfronts and reflected light. Critique, plan and 📹 (Practice Shots #4) snap again.

Notes:

Metropolitan Areas

☞ When taking pictures in the city, remember the main elements of photography, and especially these points:

- ❑ Avoid clutter in the foreground, but you need something in the foreground to draw the eye in.
- ❑ Watch out for immovable objects. Make sure they are not in the way.

📖 Read about taking pictures in cities.

✏ Make a list of all the points to remember, beginning with isolating the focal point.

☞ Look for patterns, shadows, big and little (buildings, trees), contrast (old and new), unusual shapes, interesting details.

 Practice Shots #1: take shots of the following, along with anything else you see that looks interesting:

- ❑ buildings
- ❑ people
- ❑ from rooftops (illustration A)
- ❑ down a street with the focal point (illustration B)

B *continued*

A

Metropolitan Areas

Notes:

at the other end (building, statue, door or something large) (illustrations C)

❑ up the side of a tall building (angled shot increases feeling of height) (illustration D)

❑ reflections in windows or in water (illustration E)

✏ Critique the pictures in writing or discussion.

🎥 Practice Shots #2: retake; try again.

🗁 Put both sets of pictures - the before and after - in your notebook, along with the critique.

🎥 For fun, take pictures of people in the city. Make sure the setting portrays a "city" look.

Action Shots

☞   Read about taking action pictures.

☞   Read about panning.

☞   Check Instruction Booklet for your model for hints on successful action shots.

☞   Remember the basic elements of good photography. Make a list of tips to remember in taking good action pictures.

☞   Remember to keep the subject as the focal point, while keeping in mind the Rule of Thirds.

☞   When working with moving subjects, remember to keep the subject moving *into* the picture, rather than *out of* the picture.

🎥   Practice Shots #1: take action shots with a flash and without a flash; outdoors and indoors.

✏"   Critique the action pictures in writing or discussion: what you like about the picture, what you think is wrong with the picture and ways you would remedy it the next time. Are the pictures blurry? Did you capture a feeling of action or just of blur? Is there a clear focal point? Would your pictures improve if you had a more sophisticated camera with fast-speed film? (You might be ready to broaden your knowledge and practice.)

🎥   Practice Shots #2: take more action photographs and make the corrections you suggested. Do the second shots look better? If not, try again.

🗀   Put both sets of pictures - the before and after - in your notebook, along with the critique.

Animals

Animal Pets

☞ Read about photographing pets.

☞ Preset camera (lighting, focus, flash) so you are ready when the best shot presents itself.

☞ Attract the animal's attention towards the camera with noises, a toy, bone, or food. You can also try having someone the pet knows stand where you want the animal to look while they talk to the pet.

☞ The best shots are taken on-level with the animal, not above.

☞ Set the stage or pose the animal by putting it on something or having someone hold it. You can put the pet on a pedestal, table, blanket, chair, in a tree, its house or in someone's arms.

☞ Moving subject – read about panning (see previous lessons about Action Pictures).

🎥 Practice Shots #1: using as many of the suggestions above as you can.

✏️" Critique the animal pictures in writing or discussion: what you like about the picture, what you think is wrong with the picture and ways you would remedy it the next time. Are animals easier or harder to work with than people?

🎥 Practice Shots #2: take similar pet photographs and make the corrections you suggested. Do the second shots look better? If not, try again.

📁 Put both sets of pictures - the before and after - in your notebook, along with the critique.

Animals

Zoo Animals

☞ Read about photographing animals in cages.

☞ Focus on the subject and try to get the cage to be unfocused in the foreground.

☞ Remember to check these:
- ❑ Lighting
- ❑ Subject not too far away
- ❑ Reflective surfaces while taking a flash

☞ Practice Shots #3: of zoo animals

✏" Critique the zoo pictures in writing or discussion: what you like about the picture, what you think is wrong with the picture and ways you would remedy it the next time. Did the subjects stand still for you?

📹 Practice Shots #4: if you can go back to the zoo, take the same photographs and make the corrections you suggested. Do the second shots look better? If not, try again.

📁 Put both sets of pictures - the before and after - in your notebook, along with the critique.

Animals In the Wild (at paid "safari" amusement parks or in the field)

☞ Read about taking pictures from cars

☞ Remember these:
- ❑ Clean the windows of the car before starting the journey.
- ❑ Information about panning and action shots.
- ❑ If you are in a stopped car, lean camera on window for stability.
- ❑ Telephoto lenses are fun to use if you have one. This would be an ideal opportunity to try one.

📹 Practice Shots #5: of animals in the wild.

Animals

✏️ Critique the silhouette pictures in writing: what you like about the picture, what you think is wrong with the picture and ways you would remedy it the next time.

🎥 Practice Shots #6: take similar wild animal photographs and make the corrections you suggested. Do the second shots look better? If not, try again.

🗀 Put both sets of pictures - the before and after - in your notebook, along with the critique.

☞ Read about stalking animals to photograph.

☞ When stalking animals, keep these points in mind:
- ❑ Wear colors that blend in with the surroundings - usually drab brown and green. And not *noisy* clothing or shoes (pants that *swish*, shoes that *squeak*).
- ❑ Stay downwind from the animals (wind in *your* face), so they don't pick up your scent.
- ❑ Don't make any sudden movements to frighten them away. No unnecessary noise.
- ❑ When photographing birds, hide near a bird feeder or bird bath. You can be inside a window or behind a bush. Wait for the bird to come along. And remember to **have your camera ready**.

🎥 Practice Shots #7: using the tips above.

✏️ Critique the pictures in writing: what you like about the picture, what you think is wrong with the picture and ways you would remedy it the next time.

🎥 Practice Shots #8: take similar photographs making the corrections you suggested. Do the second shots look better? If not, try again.

🗀 Put both sets of pictures - the before and after - in your notebook, along with the critique.

Special Effects

☞ Usually, when photographing a subject, you want the image to be immediately recognizable and represent the real thing. However, there are many fun and varied effects you can create with a camera. Double exposures, the use of filters and reflectors, close-ups, panorama view. Some of these are possible to duplicate without high cost. The panorama we have already tried. The reflectors we have touched on (taking pictures reflected off windows). Now, let's have some more fun.

📖 Read about using reflection to create images: mirrors, reflective balls, store windows, shiny cars and more.

✎ Come up with a list of different ways you can use reflective devices to get interesting pictures.

📹 Practice Shots #1: follow through with your list and photograph your ideas.

✎ Critique the pictures, 📹 (Practice Shots #2) take the shots again, 📁 put into notebook.

💣 Try this: have someone stand with half their body reflected in a mirror and the other half behind it. They can put their foot in the air, if they like. Take the picture. Critique and see if you can think of ways to make the photos better. 📹 (Practice Shots #3) take the shots again, 📁 put into notebook.

📖 Read about using filters in photography.

✎ Define filter as related to photography.

☞ As a reminder, never put anything on the lens of the camera. One scratch makes the camera almost unusable.

☞ A filter is basically a transparent attachment for a camera lens that is colored or tinted to alter the wavelengths of the light that project into the camera lens. Filters change the appearance or color of the image. A filter can be a store-bought glass disc or a piece of plastic

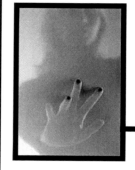

Special Effects

that fits over the front of the camera lens. There are five basic categories of alterations that filters make:

- ❑ enhance contrast by absorbing ultraviolet rays
- ❑ alter tones and values in black and white pictures
- ❑ reduce the amount of light projected into the lens
- ❑ alter the temperature of the color entering the lens (makes cool colors appear warmer, or warm tones appear cooler)
- ❑ alters the color

☞ The basic filters and uses are:
- ❑ Yellow filter: for black & white landscape pictures. The filter darkens the sky, making the clouds show up better, stronger.
- ❑ Red filter: makes a blue sky look nearly black. It is good for photographing light objects against the sky.
- ❑ Purple filter (or ultraviolet): it protects the lens from dirt and fingerprints. It also cuts down on haze - great for blue skies and ocean-side shots

💣☀️📹 Practice Shots #4: Try various colored transparent cellophane papers as filters. Or use tinted sunglasses as filters. Pieces of colored glass can also be used, just be careful of any sharp edges.

💣☀️📹 Practice Shots #5: Cut a hole in the center of a piece of colored cellophane paper to create a "color spot" filter. Start with a ½" hole. After developing the pictures, see if the hole needs to be enlarged. Good for taking portraits.

✏️ Can you think of other items you can use as colored filters?

💣☀️📹 Practice Shots #6: Try viewing through binoculars held in front of the lens. Focus and snap a picture.

💣☀️📹 Practice Shots #7: Try viewing through a microscope ocular. Focus and snap a picture.

💣☀️📹 Practice Shots #8: Take a shot through textured or patterned glass.

Special Effects

💣✶📹 Practice Shots #8: Take a shot through textured or patterned glass.

📖 Read about soft focus filters.

☞ Soft focus filters are lenses with a very fine grid engraved on the surface.

💣✶📹 Practice Shots #9: You can duplicate a soft focus filter by using a stocking (pantyhose) over the lens of your camera. Secure stocking with a rubber band. Good for snapping pictures of nighttime lights or holiday lights.

💣✶📹 Practice Shots #10: Using a separate lens, filter or piece of glass, make a swirl on the outer section of the lens with petroleum jelly. Take a cotton swab and move in a circular motion around the outer portion of the lens area. Leave the center section of the lens untouched. Take a picture through this lens, to get a swirled or moving affect.

☞ Practice Shots #11: Star filters, polarizing filters and others each have special effects they create in photographs. If this area interests you, read, explore, experiment. Find out more and have fun.

🚌 Field Trip: Find a photographer who works with special effects and filters. Ask if you can observe them at work for a specified amount of time (a few hours to a few weeks). Take notes, ask questions (after the photography session), look, observe, be aware of every filter and lens the photographer uses.

✏ Write a report about your field dtrip and record your observations while visiting with the special effects photographer. This will serve to remind you of the various technical devices used, techniques employed, preparation time and more. Discuss with your parent or teacher the length and format of the report.

Display

☞ Since you have invested your time, money & effort in taking these pictures, it would be wise to care for them properly.

📖 Read about storing and displaying photographs.

☞ There are three important points to remember in storing and displaying photographs. Keep them away from:
- ❑ dust
- ❑ dampness
- ❑ direct sunlight

☞ You can store pictures and use them in these ways. Can you think of other ways to store and use your photographs?
- ❑ Photo albums - make the arrangement of the photos in the order you took them or by grouping *like* photographs together - pictures of the same subject on the same or facing pages.
- ❑ Picture frames
- ❑ Mount pictures on colored background (mat board) with protective layer
- ❑ Greeting cards - make your own
- ❑ Calendar - make one with your pictures. Use computer software to create calendar pages, make them yourself, or use small store-bought monthly calendars at the bottom of each page. Glue photos on construction or other paper, having the picture relate to the month shown (summer photos for summer months). You can use a piece of ribbon, rings, comb-binding or staples to hold the calendar together at the top. Use rubber stamps, pretty stickers or felt-tip markers to make each page more attractive and festive.

Notes:

Using the Skill

☞ There are many chances to use your photography hobby while still in school. Many times these will be volunteer positions (unpaid), unless you make prior arrangements.
- ❑ school or homeschool yearbook photographer
- ❑ take pictures for your school, church or homeschool newsletter
- ❑ local newspapers sometimes hire high school students to cover local events, especially of activities with their age-group like sports events, concerts, field trips, rallies
- ❑ use your photographs as graphics to illustrate reports or written assignments

☞ If you are interested in making a living in the field of photography, there are a variety of different career opportunities. Decide which area of photography you enjoy the most, and what each of these suggestions require. By matching interest and ability with need, you get a long-lasting, enjoyable career. You might make arrangements to spend some time observing and helping people in your chosen area of interest.
- ❑ Photographer
  - ❑ Special occasions
  - ❑ Newspaper
  - ❑ Magazines
  - ❑ Nature photographer
- ❑ Film maker
- ❑ Video cameraman
- ❑ Television cameraman
- ❑ X-ray technician
- ❑ Film developer
- ❑ Sales of cameras, equipment & supplies
- ❑ Camera repairman
- ❑ Photography factory-worker (make equipment or supplies)

✎ Can you think of more careers in photography? Make a list.

Notes:

Sharpening the Skill

☞ Photography Clubs are found in schools, at youth clubs, and in home-school group settings. If you can't find one, then you might consider starting your own.
- ❑ Decide how and where to advertise (in camera shops, at local schools, in grocery stores and youth clubs).
- ❑ Local newspapers love to advertise new groups (perhaps even for free), or they may choose to write a story about it.
- ❑ Choose and confirm a date, time and place.
- ❑ If you invite a professional photographer to speak at the first meeting, it will draw more attendance.
- ❑ Your Local Library might be able to help you find local groups or beginner's classes or competitions. Or they can help advertise your new group.

Other ideas for the meeting are:
- ❑ You can discuss how to take better pictures
- ❑ You can give ideas for contests, and information about competitions
- ❑ You will get free advice and critique of pictures and techniques

Online

Websites, Chat Groups, Online Resources

The online world is tentative and transitory. What is here today, could very well be gone tomorrow. These listings were available in 2007.

A word of caution about using the online world for the subject of "photography." When we were researching the topic, many unacceptable websites came up in the listings. We have since made the filtering system on our browser more restrictive. Just please use caution if you go searching. And don't let children search alone! The websites listed here were looked through, and we found nothing questionable about them. *We cannot guarantee them, nor any links off of these websites.* Our suggestions are for an adult to view the websites first, and to stick with the well-known names and sites.

There is a lot of information, hints, tidbits, suggestions, examples and more on these websites. They are chock-full of helps.

Enjoy riding the surf!

- 💻 *Life Magazine* website: The magazine that pioneered photojournalism has re-imaged itself for cyberspace. http://pathfinder.com/Life/

- 💻 *Time Life Magazine*: photo essays   http://www.pathfinder.com/photo/index.html

- 💻 **Amateur Photographers Association**: http://www.photo association.com/

- 💻 **Friends of Photography**: Interesting exhibit information & books to order from the library http://www.friendsofphotography.org/

- 💻 **Panorama Pictures**: http://lcweb2.loc.gov/ammem/pnhtml/

- 💻 **Nikon**: http://www.nikon-image.com/eng/

Online

🖥 **Kodak**: http://www.kodak.com/

🖥 **Polaroid**: http://www.polaroid.com/index.html

🖥 **Society for Photographic Education**: http://www.spenational.org/

🖥 Contests advertised on the internet: http://www.picture.com/

🖥 Outdoor Shots http://www.rdsphoto.com/

🖥 The **Photographic Society of America** (PSA) is the largest organization of its kind in the world, bringing together amateur and professionals in all the varied fields of photography. http://www.psaphoto.org/

Magazines

Photo Traveller
P.O. Box 39912, Los Angeles, CA 90039, 800-417-4680, 323-660-8600, FAX 323-660-0473, phototravel@phototravel.com
http://phototravel.com/ptn.htm

Shutterbug Magazine
5211 S. Washington Ave., Titusville, Fl USA 32780
Phone: (407) 269-3212 Fax: (407) 269-2025
http://www.shutterbug.net/

Life Magazine
(See information under "Online"). Order a free trial issue by calling *Life Magazine* Customer Service at 1-800-621-6000 or writing to LIFE, P.O. Box 60001, Tampa, FL 33660-0001. Please specify that you would like to take advantage of the free trial issue offer from LIFE and include reference code LIBCQN1.

Time Magazine
To Order By Phone, call 1-800-367-0168 (credit card orders) (There is concern about ordering this magazine for children, because of its adult topics and differing views. However, the photographs are supposedly award-winning. Please make your own decision.)

Associations

✉ **Alpa Cameras:** ASMP (American Society of Media Photographers), Washington Pk, Suite 502, 14 Washington Road, Princeton Junction, NJ 08550 (609) 799-8300

✉ **Friends of Photography**, PO Box 500, Carmel, CA 93921, (415) 495-7000

✉ **International Center of Photography** (ICP): 1130 Fifth Avenue, New York, NY 10128, (212) 860-1781

✉ **NANPA (North American Nature Photography Association)** 10200 W 44th Avenue, Suite 304, Wheat Ridge, CO 80033 (303) 422-8527

✉ **National Free Lance Photographers Association** 60 E State Street, Doyleston, PA 18901

✉ **National Photographic Society:** 433 Route 130, Sandwich, MA 02563

✉ **National Press Photographers Association:** 3200 Croasdaile Dr., #306, Durham, NC 27705 (800) 289-6772

✉ **National Stereoscopic Association:** P.O. Box 14801, Columbus, OH 43214

✉ **Nikon Historical Society:** Photographic Manufacturing and Distributors Association (PMDA), 866 United Nations Plaza, Suite 436, New York, NY 10017   (212) 688-3520

✉ **Photo Marketing Association:** 3000 Picture Place, Jackson, MI 49201 (517) 788-8100

✉ **Photographic Society of America** (PSA): 3000 United Founders Blvd., #103, Oklahoma City, OK 73114 (405) 843-1437 *The world wide association of advanced photographers from all over the world with approximately 6,000 members.*

✉ **Underwater Photographic Society:** PO Box 2401, Culver City, CA 90231

✉ **Wedding and Portrait Photographers International** (WPPI): 1312 Lincoln Blvd., Santa Monica, CA 90406   (310) 451-0090

✉ **White House News Photographers Association** (WHNPA): 7119 Ben Franklin Station, Washington, DC 20014   (202) 785-5230

Vocabulary

Camera Types
adjustable camera
automatic camera
camera
instant camera
single lens reflex
view camera

Camera Parts
auto winder
diaphragm
magazine
range finder
shutter
shutter speed
viewfinder

Lens & Film
adjustable focus lens
aperture
ASA
autofocus
automatic aperture
cartridge
cassette
close-up
close-up lens
color negative film
color print film
darkroom
double exposure
enlargement
enlarger
expiration date
exposure
f-stop
film holder
film magazine
film speed
filter
fish-eye lens
fixed focus lens

infinity
lens
lens cleaner
lens opening
macro lens
magnification
micro lens
negative
print
process
record
telephoto lens
through-the-lens
time exposure
transparent
twin-lens reflex
wide-angle lens
zoom lens

Composition & Focal Point
background
blur
center of interest
composition
depth of field (DOF)
depth of focus
focal length
focal point
focus
focusing
foreground
frame
framing
image
picture area
rule of thirds
subject image

Lighting
artificial lighting
automatic electronic flash
available light

background light
back lighting
bounce lighting
contrast
existing light
fill
fill-in light
flash
flashbar
flashcube
flash unit
flat lighting
flipflash
front lighting
hot shoe
lighting
light meter
magicube
natural light
pink-eye
red-eye
side lighting
top lighting

Point of View & Angles
aerial perspective
angle of view
camera angle
field of view
perspective
viewpoint

Photographing People
candid photograph
candid shot
portrait
portrait lighting

Landscape & Panorama
panning
panorama
panoramic camera

Book List

There are many books on photography. While we did not view every single one available, we did read and enjoy these. The library should have these titles or great substitutions. Listed here by author, title, and Dewey Decimal Number. ("J" refers to the Juvenile section of the library - "Kid's Area.")

- Bostrom, Roald: A Look Inside Cameras J771.3 BOS

- Laycock, George. The Complete Beginner's Guide to J770.28 LAY

- Forbes, Robin. Click, A First Camera Book J770 FOR

- Morgan, Terri & Shmuel Thaler Photography: Take Your Best Shot J771 MOR

- Smith, Peter The First Photography Book J770.28 SMI

- Watts, Barrie & Jonathan Hilton A First Guide to Photography J770.233 WAT

- Hawksby, Peter & Jane Chisholm Beginner's Guide to Cameras & Photography J770 HAW

- Haines, George The Young Photographer's Handbook J770 HAI

- Jacobs, Lou, Jr. Instant Photography J770.28 JAC

- Craven, John & John Wasley Young Photographer J770 CRA

- Vlitos, Roger Taking Photos J770.28 VLI

- Leen, Nina Taking Pictures J770.28 L

- Osinski, Christine I Can Be A Photographer J770.23 OS

- Freeman, Tony Photography A New True Book J770 Fre

- Gibbons, Gail Click! A Book about Cameras and Taking Pictures J771 GIB

Kym's Konstruction Kit is fairly simple to use, just read the explanation to understand the system.

Below is a sample of the bottom of each lesson plan page. Write notes to yourself in the box to help you remember. Every resource we need for a particular lesson, I write on this one page. It saves me having to remember where I wrote it down, where the picture is, what book it was in and all. So, if you write it all down on the bottom of the page, it will help you be organized!

A sample of the top of each lesson plan page is on the following page. The number in each boxed explanation correlates to the number on the lesson plan sample. There is a line attaching the two. Beginning at ❶ read the explanations and look at the sample.

The lesson plans are on the following pages. If you would like to change a lesson plan, or set up your own - for one or more days - there is a blank copy of the lesson plan on page 78 for you to use. Make the schedule and lesson plans work for you and your family. Fit it into your schedule and needs.

If you need to have film developed, then plan the unit accordingly. Perhaps working on the unit only 2 days per week, to have time for film development - or find a one-hour photo processing shop near your home!

Have fun as you learn how to take better pictures!   *Kym Wright*

Bottom of lesson plan page:

Daily: read related material
answer questions
define vocabulary words

PH=Photography

These are the things we do every day we are working on *Photography*. Defining and working with the vocabulary words helps the student internalize the information and understand the books & experts.

The rest of the boxed area is for you to write down videos to watch, materials to gather, resources you need, field trips for that topic, or other notes to yourself. This is to help keep you organized with everything on one page.

The **Legend** explains the abbreviations in the lesson plans. PH=*Photography*, this curriculum.
You may add other abbreviations of resources used often.

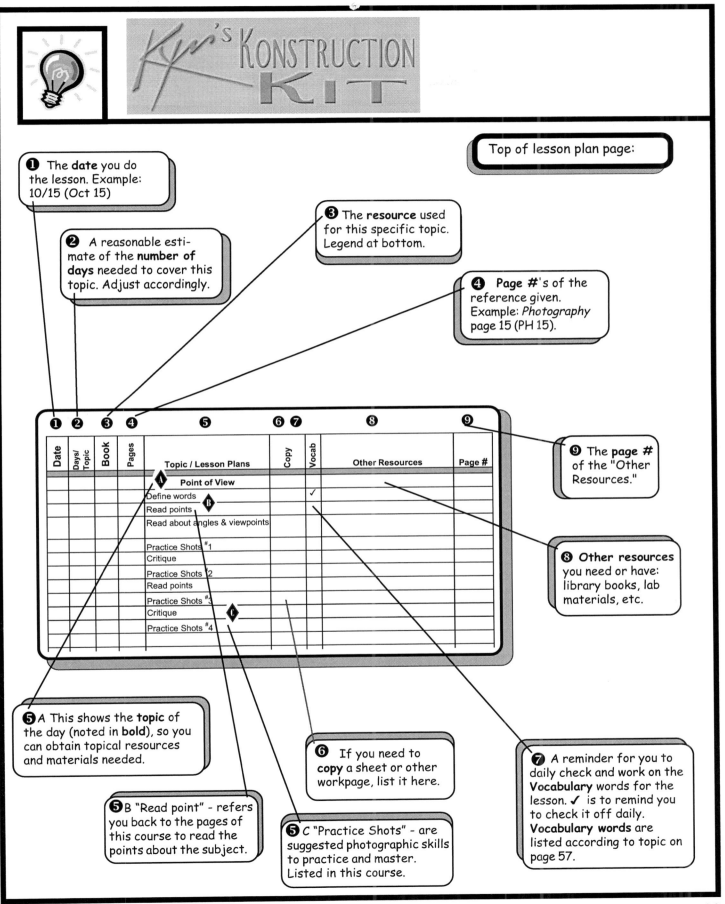

Kim's Konstruction Kit

Top of lesson plan page:

❶ The **date** you do the lesson. Example: 10/15 (Oct 15)

❷ A reasonable estimate of the **number of days** needed to cover this topic. Adjust accordingly.

❸ The **resource** used for this specific topic. Legend at bottom.

❹ **Page #**'s of the reference given. Example: *Photography* page 15 (PH 15).

❾ The **page #** of the "Other Resources."

❽ **Other resources** you need or have: library books, lab materials, etc.

❺A This shows the **topic** of the day (noted in **bold**), so you can obtain topical resources and materials needed.

❺B "Read point" - refers you back to the pages of this course to read the points about the subject.

❻ If you need to **copy** a sheet or other workpage, list it here.

❺C "Practice Shots" - are suggested photographic skills to practice and master. Listed in this course.

❼ A reminder for you to daily check and work on the **Vocabulary** words for the lesson. ✓ is to remind you to check it off daily. **Vocabulary words** are listed according to topic on page 57.

❶ Date	❷ Days/Topic	❸ Book	❹ Pages	❺ Topic / Lesson Plans	❻ Copy	❼ Vocab	❽ Other Resources	❾ Page #
				Point of View				
				Define words		✓		
				Read points				
				Read about angles & viewpoints				
				Practice Shots #1				
				Critique				
				Practice Shots #2				
				Read points				
				Practice Shots #3				
				Critique				
				Practice Shots #4				

Date	Days/ Topic	Book	Pages	Topic / Lesson Plans	Copy	Vocab	Other Resources	Page #
				Set up Digitial Camera demo				
	1			**Introduction**		✓		
		PH	4	Read "How to Use"	p6-8			
		PH	4	Learn symbol definitions	p6			
			5	Set up Notebook	p7			
	1		5	Gather materials	p.7-8			
		PH	7	Read "Outline"	p.9-11			
	2-3	PH	10	**Camera Parts & Types**		✓		
			10	Read about camera parts	p13			
			11	Locate and name the parts of your camera	p14			
		PH	12	Read about camera types	p14			
				Look at pictures of other types of cameras, noting different parts, placements and styles				
				Draw a picture of your camera; label the parts				
				Read about the history of cameras	↓			

Daily: read related material
answer questions
define vocabulary words

PH=Photography Unit

Date	Days/ Topic	Book	Pages	Topic / Lesson Plans	Copy	Vocab	Other Resources	Page #
	1	PH	13	**Digital Cameras**		✓		
				Read about digital cameras	p15			
			14	Visit websites	p16			
				Learn how to use	p16			
	1			Digital Camera demo	p17			
	1	PH	16	**Lenses**		✓		
				Read about the basic types of lenses	p18			
				Discuss the various types, how they function, purpose & use				
				Read about the various topics listed				
				Note lens type on your camera(s)				
				Define the various special lenses				
	1			Field Trip	↓			

Daily: read related material
answer questions
define vocabulary words

PH=Photography Unit

Date	Days/Topic	Book	Pages	Topic / Lesson Plans	Copy	Vocab	Other Resources	Page #
	3	PH	17	**Film**		✓		
				Define film	p19			
				Read about film				
				List various types of film				
				Field Trip				
				Explanation paragraph				
				Read about film speed				
				Explanation paragraph				
				Learn how to put film in your camera				
				Definitions	↓	✓		
			18	Read "Lens & Film"	p20			
				Make Pinhole Camera	p21-22			
				Answer questions	p22			
				Read information				
				Experiment with eyes				
				Write paragraph	↓			

Daily: read related material
answer questions
define vocabulary words

PH=Photography Unit

Date	Days/ Topic	Book	Pages	Topic / Lesson Plans	Copy	Vocab	Other Resources	Page #
	6	PH	21	**Composition**				
			23	Read Kodak's Top Ten Techniques	p23			
				Visit website				
				Read about focusing the camera				
			21	Read about camera views	↓			
			23	Practice Shots #1	p24			
				Practice Shots #2				
				Practice Shots #3	↓			
			23	Rule of Thirds	p25			
				Read about Focal Point				
				Read about Foreground				
				View pictures	↓			
				Practice shots #4	p26			
			23	Read about angles & depth				
				Practice Shots #5				
				Critique				
				Practice Shots #6	↓			

Daily: read related material
answer questions
define vocabulary words

PH=Photography Unit

Date	Days/ Topic	Book	Pages	Topic / Lesson Plans	Copy	Vocab	Other Resources	Page #
	3	PH	25	**Lighting**		✓		
			25	Read "Lighting"	p27			
				Read about lighting in other resources				
				Define words		✓		
				Remedy situations				
				Equipment information				
				Visit website	↓			
				Read about flash systems	p28			
				Define words		✓		
				Learn to use your flash system				
				Read about cautions with flashes				
				Write list				
				Practice Shots #1				
				Critique				
				Practice Shots #2	↓			

Daily: read related material
answer questions
define vocabulary words

PH=Photography Unit

Photography

Date	Days/ Topic	Book	Pages	Topic / Lesson Plans	Copy	Vocab	Other Resources	Page #
	4	PH	27	**Point of View**		✓		
				Define words p29				
				Read points				
				Read about angles & viewpoints				
				Practice Shots #1				
				Critique				
				Practice Shots #2 p.30				
				Read points (sun)				
				Practice Shots #3				
				Critique				
				Practice Shots #4				

Daily: read related material
answer questions
define vocabulary words

PH=Photography Unit

Date	Days/ Topic	Book	Pages	Topic / Lesson Plans	Copy	Vocab	Other Resources	Page #
	5	PH	29	**People**				
				Read about photographing people P31				
				Read points				
				List				
				Practice Shots #1				
				Practice Shots #2				
				Critique p32				
				Read points				
				Explain rules				
				Practice Shots #3				
				Descriptions				
				Read about subject focus				
				Read points				
				Practice Shots #4 p.33				
				Critique				
				Read points				
				Practice Shots #5				
				Critique				

Daily: read related material
answer questions
define vocabulary words

PH=Photography Unit

Date	Days/ Topic	Book	Pages	Topic / Lesson Plans	Copy	Vocab	Other Resources	Page #
	4	PH	32	**Portraits**				
				Read points _p34_				
				Practice Shots #1				
				Critique				
				Practice Shots #2 _p35_				
				Read points about self portraits				
				Read about taking self portraits				
				Practice Shots #3				
				Critique				
				Practice Shots #4				
	3	PH	34	**Silhouettes**				
				Define _p36_				
				Read points				
				Read about taking silhouette photographs				
				Read the different methods				
				Practice Shots #1				
				Critique				
				Practice Shots #2				

Daily: read related material
answer questions
define vocabulary words

PH=Photography Unit

Date	Days/ Topic	Book	Pages	Topic / Lesson Plans	Copy	Vocab	Other Resources	Page #
	4	PH	35	**Group Pictures**				
				Read points p.37				
				Practice Shots #1				
				Practice Shots #2				
				Critique				
				View group pictures p.38				
				Critique yours and others'				
				Practice Shots #3				
				Critique				
				Read points				
				Practice Shots #4				
				Critique				
				Practice Shots #5				

Daily: read related material
answer questions
define vocabulary words

PH=Photography Unit

Date	Days/Topic	Book	Pages	Topic / Lesson Plans	Copy	Vocab	Other Resources	Page #
	4	PH	37	**Landscape**				
				Read points	p39			
				Look at pictures of landscapes				
				Read points				
				Practice Shots #1				
				Critique	↓			
				Practice Shots #2	p40			
				Read about Panorama Pictures				
				Visit website				
				Read points	↓			
				Practice Shots #3	p41			
				Critique				
				Practice Shots #4	↓			
	4	PH	40	**Patterns & Waterfront**				
				Read about pattern & texture pictures	p42			
				Read points				
				Practice Shots #1				
				Critique				
				Practice Shots #2				
				Read about waterfront photographs				
				Read points				
				Practice Shots #3				
				Critique				
				Practice Shots #4	↓			

Daily: read related material
answer questions
define vocabulary words

PH=Photography Unit

Date	Days/ Topic	Book	Pages	Topic / Lesson Plans	Copy	Vocab	Other Resources	Page #
	2	PH	41	**Metropolitan Areas**	p43			
				Read points				
				Read about taking City Pictures				
				List				
				Practice Shots #1	↓			
				Critique	p44			
				Practice Shots #2	↓			
	4	PH	43	**Action Shots**	p45			
				Read about taking action shots				
				Read about panning				
				Read points				
				Practice Shots #1				
				Critique				
				Practice Shots #2	↓			

Daily: read related material
answer questions
define vocabulary words

PH=Photography Unit

Date	Days/ Topic	Book	Pages	Topic / Lesson Plans	Copy	Vocab	Other Resources	Page #
	9	PH	44	**Animals**				
				Read about photographing pets	p 46			
				Read points				
				Practice Shots #1				
				Critique				
				Practice Shots #2				
				Read about photographing caged animals	p 47			
				Read points				
				Practice Shots #3				
				Critique				
				Practice Shots #4				
				Read about photographing animals in the "wild"				
				Read about photographing from a car				
				Read points				
				Practice Shots #5				
				Critique	p 48			
				Practice Shots #6				
				Read about stalking animals for photographing				
				Read points				
				Practice Shots #7				
				Critique				
				Practice Shots #8				

Daily: read related material
answer questions
define vocabulary words

PH=Photography Unit

Date	Days/ Topic	Book	Pages	Topic / Lesson Plans	Copy	Vocab	Other Resources	Page #
	7	PH	47	**Special Effects**				
				Read points	p49			
				Read about special effects				
				List				
				Practice Shots #1				
				Critique				
				Practice Shots #2				
				Read points				
				Practice Shots #3				
				Definitions	✓			
				Read about filters	✓ 2			
				Read points	↓ 49/50			
				Practice Shots #4	p50			
				Practice Shots #5				
				Practice Shots #6				
				Practice Shots #7				
				Practice Shots #8	↓			
				Practice Shots #9	p51			
				Critique & experiment more				
				Read about soft focus filters				
				Practice Shots #10				
				Practice Shots #11				
				Read about other special filters				
				Practice Shots #12				
				Field Trip				
				Report	↓			

Daily: read related material
answer questions
define vocabulary words

PH=Photography Unit

Date	Days/ Topic	Book	Pages	Topic / Lesson Plans	Copy	Vocab	Other Resources	Page #
		PH	50	**Display**				
				Read points	*p52*			
				Read about storing and displaying photographs				
				Read points				
	1			Make a photo album				
	1			Put photos in frames, or make your own frames				
	1			Mount pictures				
	2			Make greeting cards				
	2-3			Make a calendar	↓			
	2	PH	51	**Using the Skill**	*p 53*			
				Read points				
				Read about career opportunities in photography				
				Add to the list				
				Field Trips to observe				
				Join or start a club				
				Practice the skill	↓			

Daily: read related material
answer questions
define vocabulary words

PH=Photography Unit

Date	Days/Topic	Book	Pages	Topic / Lesson Plans	Copy	Vocab	Other Resources	Page #

Daily: read related material
answer questions
define vocabulary words

PH=Photography Unit

Photography

Notes:

_____

Notes:

In the *Women: Living Life on Purpose Series*, we have CD sets and companion books on various topics.

In her talks, Kym casts a vision of motherhood, being a wife, organizing the house, and loving it all. She shares scripture, practical solutions, and all the warm stories she's known for. Each topic is well researched with biblical concordances, commentaries and the Bible itself, along with information from the experts.

Come join Kym as she shares her heart for women to live life on purpose.

Children & Chores
3-CD Set & Companion Book

From a "let's enjoy ourselves and have fun" and the work not getting done, to a more organized family life, join Kym as she shares her journey in teaching her eight children how to work and choose a good attitude about it.

She talks about children's chores from a biblical perspective, casting a vision of why we want to teach our children to work. What the Bible has to say about work and training our children. Kym helps you establish the reasons to teach our children to work.

Work attitudes are discussed – ours and our offspring's – and how to create the plan with chore charts.

Family Meals
3-CD Set & Companion Book

Research shows when adults and children eat together . . .children do better in school, they have fewer behavior problems, and they like talking with the adults in their lives. Teens are less apt to smoke, use alcohol or drugs and family values and traditions and traditions are passed on.

Studies indicate that meals are more nutritious and healthful, food dollars stretch further, time is better utilized because the family only cooks one meal, and many times the family is involved in meal preparation. Are we talking about "The Waltons," or will this work for me and my family? Join Kym as she shares the vision of the **Family Meal**, its importance, how to plan meals and shop for groceries with great ease, and how each family can create special times around the table, with just a bit of preparation.

Moms Mentoring Moms

This series came about through Bible Studies Kym held in her home, for young mothers and single women. When they finished our study on Children and Chores, and on Family Meals they asked Kym to teach them a short study on Titus 2. Many call these verses the "Older women teach the younger women verses." Kym just calls them the "Moms Mentoring Moms" scriptures.

What do these verses mean? How do they apply to my life today? Can we really find practical guidance in these scriptures? We'll answer these questions and more.

Kym shares the Don't's, the Do's and the Why of Titus 2: How are we to live? If I don't drink, then how can that portion of the verse apply to me which says not to be enslaved to much wine? With a strongly biblical basis, and many of her heart-warming stories, Kym shares the very practical ways we can live out these verses in everyday life. Without being Superwoman, and with the husband and children we each have.

Come and join Kym as she shares about Moms Mentoring Moms.

Creating Creativity
1-CD Set

"An idea can turn to dust or magic, depending on the talent that rubs against it."
~ Bill Bernbach, advertising expert

Why do we, as moms, want to invest our time and money in art projects? Especially when we already have so much on our plates. Why would we want to even delve into this expanse of art? Where the lines are blurred, and we're not even experts?

Many moms feel that they have the proverbial "2 left feet" when it comes to art. To set a foundation for learning, Kym references some of the greatest creative forces in our world: Einstein, Bill Gates, the founder of Poloroid Corporation, artists, educators, philsophers, and doctors. All agree that creativity is a vital element in life, and teaching it to our children is integral to their future success.

Join Kym as she shares ways to teach our children creativity – even if that trait is not ours. She gives ideas, resources, lists and more to help you appear more creative, and to help our children accomplish it.

Gift of Goals
1-CD Set

Research indicates those who write their goals out, 95% of them will reach their goals. The Bible gives reason to plan our lives in several places: Proverbs 29:18 "Where there is no vision, the people perish." And Isaiah 32:8, "But the noble man devises noble plans; and by noble plans he stands."

Planning keeps us from acting in haste – from being so spontaneous that it gets us in trouble. Or that we flit from this to that, and never settle in on any one thing. And how do we share this with our children? How do we help them live by goals, rather than just responding and reacting to life?

Join Kym as she shares her journey of the Gift of Goals: the areas to set them in, how to reassess and how often, and how to help our children dream big, and break these into smaller, bite-size pieces.

Magazine Article Writing
6-CD Set & Session Notes

Let the story inside you become a blessing to others

A course on getting published

Turn your dreams into bylines and help yourself to a bright future as a magazine writer. If you're a determined writer – experienced or not, this class will provide you with the skills you need to get published.

This course is about how to write for magazines, getting published and to broaden your scope while helping yourself to a bright future as a magazine writer. Learn to share your stories and testimony, God's blessing in your life, and encouragement to others. You will learn how to find interesting ideas and angles for articles to locate suitable markets, how to research and write query letters, article structure and submitting articles – all this and more.

This series will jump start your career. You'll learn plenty of powerful brainstorming techniques designed to practically write every article for you: where to get ideas, how to structure your articles, how to find markets, and how to make queries and submissions. We'll take a closer look at the magazine editorial process and how you can make that work to your advantage by focusing your writing for a particular audience. You'll learn how to approach major market magazines, how to get past the slush pile, how to follow up until you have a sale and how to follow through until you have completed the assignment satisfactorily. Then we'll discuss making the most use of your time: time management, how to resell your article, and how to write a second article from the same research.

Kym is an energetic and encouraging speaker. She has spoken to many groups including MOPS or Mothers of PreSchoolers groups, state homeschool conventions, local homeschool groups, Rotary and Kiwanis Clubs, Civic Organizations, church groups, women's events and seminars, teen groups, and more!

Kym is the mother of eight homeschooled children. She and her husband, Mark, have homeschooled since the mid 80s. They have graduated four students who are attending college and holding down jobs, internships and apprenticeships in their chosen fields.

Sharing her love of motherhood and homeschooling on **The 700 Club**, on **radio** shows and in her writing, **her passion shows . . . and it's contagious**.

Kym is author of the **Learn & Do Unit Studies** and *Women: Living Life on Purpose*, a mommy-primer helping women become the best wife, mother and friend they can be. She has been the editor of various local, regional and statewide newsletters, as well as having her articles published in many homeschool publications, including *Homeschooling Today, The Old Schoolhouse,* and *Practical Homeschooling* and now publishes an online magazine **The Mother's Heart**.

Kym writes to encourage moms in very practical, hands-on ways making the philosophical very workable. She shares the love of raising children, teaching preschoolers, being the mother of older children, homeschooling and the privilege of helping our children find God's call in their lives.

Visit her websites:

www.KymWright.com
www.Learn-and-Do.com
www.The-Mothers-Heart.com
www.Living-Life-on-Purpose.com

To contact Kym to speak for your event: info@KymWright.com or Kym Wright, PO Box 81124, Conyers, Ga 30013.

The Mother's Heart — Back Issues

#1 Aug 96

Vol 1 #1: Aug '96: Letters From Your Heart; Coming Home (Kym's journey from business to staying home); Parenting Power: The Foundation; Thinking about Adoption; Passing On Harvard; Life on Schedule; Becoming the Family Herbalist; Keeping up with the Jones'; Miracle of Morgan; When Daddy Travels.

#2 Nov 96

Vol 1 #2: Nov '96: Life Influencers; Respect; What Pushes Your Buttons?; Adoption: HomeStudy and Kym's Experience; Infertility... and God; Literature: Literacy or Legacy?; Rising Early; Natural Pregnancy; Home HairCutting; A Medical Couple Looks at God's Family Planning; Families ... like Quilts; The Hospitable Home; I Don't Know How You Do It!; Cows; Milk; Cheesemaking.

#3 Feb 97

Vol 1 #3: Feb '97: A Joyful Mother; Obedience; Who's In Charge Anyway?; Adoption: Consents; Breast Infections; Straight Talk; Finding Extraordinary in Ordinary; Male's HairCut; Children's Chores; Choosing Contentment; Herbs: Mommy Diagnostics; Ready for a Baby; Million Dollar Family; Loneliness; SuperMom!

#4 May 97

Vol 1 #4: May '97: Country Chic!; Her Children Rise Up and Call Her Blessed; From Your Heart; Responsibility; First Things First!; Birth Father's Rights; Why Adopt?; Pregnant With #10!; Learning To Trust: Mom of 11; Mothering on Purpose; Children's Chores (part 2); Blank Chore Chart; Internet & Heart; Cheap Dec! & Painting Verdé; Herbs: PMS: Pre-Menstral Syndrome:

#5 Aug 97

What Is It?

Vol 2 #5: Aug '97: Bits 'N Pieces; Behind Every Successful Mother; Discerning Vital Life Principles: Mate Maintenance; Biracial Adoption; His Way; Infertility: Desire of My Heart; Private Decisions; Color Blind; Autumn Garden; Our Family of 14 Children; How Can We Trust God More For Family Planning?; Lavish Living; Kitchen ShortKuts; Our New Kitchen; Female's Blunt HairCut; Garlic Bag; Pattern Notebooks; Older Siblings; Staying Home While Sick; Library: @ Your Service, Onsite & Form; Bird Unit Study.

#6 Nov 97

Vol 2 #6: Nov '97: A Higher Education; Family Life; Spanking; Wiring 101; Discussing Adoption Concerns; Gentle Schedules; Blending Natural & Modern Medicine; His Queen; My King; Infertility & God; VP to Play Dough Mom; Scrunchies; Alter a Bathrobe; Children's Measurements & Forms.

#7 Feb 98

Vol 2 #7: Feb '98: Dealing with Disappointment; Family Fun; Capturing Their Heart; Wiring 102; Open & Closed Adoption; Dominoes!; Mother's Peace; From Australia; Finding Time; Baking Bread; Orange Raisin Bread; Meal Preparation; Chicken Dishes; Incubating Eggs; Shutting Down the Complaint Dept.

#8 May 98

Vol 2 #8: May '98: Faith or Denial?; A Home Much-Loved; Capturing Their Heart; Charting a Life Course; Adoption '98; Double Blessing; More Children ~ Adoption?; Herbs; Eating Better: The Course; Preschool Basket; School Time-Management & Form; Journey to

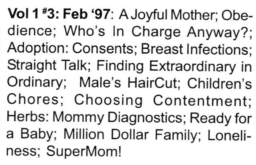

#9 Aug 98

#10 Nov 98

#11 Feb 99

#12 May 99

#13 Aug 99

Contentment; Decorating Notebook; If We Listen.

Vol 3 #9: Aug '98: A Matter of the Heart; The Harvest; Charting A Life Course; When Baby Dies in Your Womb; Recipe Experimentation; Eating Better ; Beef Dishes; Tips & Tricks; Creating Creativity; More Fun Stuff Ideas!; Once Upon A Time: Child Abuse; A Love for our Children; Trust; "Spoil"; Why are Good Books So Important; The Rest Can Wait; Women: Living Life on Purpose

Vol 3 #10: Nov '98: Children's Life Goals; The Power of the Spirit; Charting A Life Course, Pt 3; Garden of Health; Making Good Better; Faith; Growing In Grace; In Sickness or In Health; Preschool Literature; Schooling Many; One Man's Twaddle; School Organization; The Wall; Committed or Obligated? Botany; Joys of Staying Home; Ambassador of Motherhood

Vol 3 #11: Feb '99: Moving & Change; Mighty in Spirit; Adolescence; From White to Whole; Longing for an Open Womb; Adoption; Homeschooling & Organization; 'Net Connected; Correspondence College; Blessing & Dressing; Love Letter; A Journal Entry; Counting the Cost; Home & Ministry.

Vol 3 #12: May '99: Coming Home ... Again; Quiet Life; Joyful In Spirit; Children are a Blessing; Eating Better: Y2K & Beyond; Hyperchilderemia; Interstate Adoption; Raising Biological & Adopted Kids; Gentle Beauty; Preparation & Organization; Homeschooling Special Needs Children; Dean to Mom; The Professional Woman I Married; Stepping Up Your Child's Space; Scripture Memorization; A Word Kindly Spoken

Vol 4 #13: Aug '99: Standing Watch; Progress; Adolescence; Four Food Storage Plans; Menopause; Family Fitness Fun; Nausea Remedies; Healthy Granola; International Adoption; Adoption & Others; The Wait; Growing in Grace; Is the Husband Enough?; The

#14 Nov 99

#15 Feb 00

#16 May 00

#17 Aug 00

#18 Nov 00

Waltons Revisited; Classified Ads; Press On; Letting Go; A Woman of Virtue; G.E.R.M. Warfare!

Vol 4 #14: Nov '99: Maintaining the Cover; "I Will"; The Father's Blessing; Is the Husband Enough? Pt 2; Grain Mills; Immuno-Woes; Teenage Birth-mothers; Wrong Reasons to Adopt; Babies Come in Many Ways; Quilting 101; Bringing Your Heart Home; Smiley Face; Older Mom; She Rises Before Dawn... to pray; Submitting; Creation Science; Good Books; Photography Unit

Vol 4 #15: Feb '00: Equipping for Excellence, Working Women, Dating/ Courtship Parameters, Settling Family Convictions, Pastry Grains, Having Healthier Children, Regaining Pre-Pregnancy Figure, Our Story of Grace (Adoption), Time Management, Homemaker or Housewife?, Learning Takes Humility, Scrapbooking, Good Books, Making Units (Studies) Yours; Scripture Memorization... Psalm 91, New Unit: Flower Arranging & Wreaths

Vol 4 #16: May '00: Discernment; Dailyness; The *Family Pow-Wow*; How Do I Get My Husband to Lead?; Grain Variety for Quick Bread; Too Tired to be Exhausted?; Getting Started in Adoption; Honoring My Husband; Finally ... Children; Moving; Titus 2:4-5 — What Does It Really Mean?; Building up Child's Dreams; Homeschooling with Preschoolers; Why We Homeschool

Vol 5 #17: Aug '00: Music & Our Children; Brown Rice; Defeating Depression Naturally; Adoption Protection; Foster Parenting; Vaccinate or Not?; Stretch Travel Dollar; Unequally Yoked; LifeGuard Mom; Love Letter; Chemistry; Dissection, Autism, PDD & Celaic Disease; Recipes; Unit Study Answers from Authors

Vol 5 #18: Nov '00: Shepherding; Count Your Blessings; Basketball, Football & Music; Coaching Tight; Thanksgiving Favorites; Defeating Depression, Pt 2; Candida Yeast; Trusting the Creator; Foster Parenting; Shepherd's Crook;

#19 Feb 01

Adoption Story; Children ... a Gift; Spiritual Housecleaning; Wright Photo Gallery

Vol 5 #19: Feb '01: Serving Others; Unsaved Husbands; Whole Grain Crepes; ADD / ADHD; Bed-Wetting; Candida Questions; Weigh Down Update; Loving Baby Doe; Foster Care Resources; Tightwad Resolutions; Rising & Time with Husband: Q&A; Dream House; Special Children & Special Moms; Tag-A-Long Meals; Recipes; Baby Showers

#20 May 01

Vol 5 #20: May '01: Good-bye; An Engagement Story; Friends! Really?; Pasta Salad Italian; Cancer Prevention Tips; Cook Books; ; Keeping Our Arms Open; Becoming Your Child's Advocate; Adopting Your Foster Child; Sincerely Wondering; Frugal & Organized; Magazines; House & Garden; IEP: easy as PIE

#21 Feb 05

Vol 6 #21: Feb 05: Some Answers: A Love Letter; E-World; Catching up with the Wrights; Whole Grains: 2-Stage Process; Whole Wheat Bread; Moms Mentoring Moms; Grace in Teen Relations; Values; Empowering the Pastor's Wife; Adoption: My Spiritual Journey; Teaching Art at Home; Making Unit Studies Yours; Creation Science; Science Activities for Children; America's Junior Miss; Keepers at Home

#22 April 05

Vol 6 #22: April 05: Husband, Father, Protector: Destroyer of Lies; Purring & Italy; Dairy Dilemma; Bread-U-Cation; Awakening Love Too Soon; The Joy of Motherhood; The Expert Enabler; Finding Agreement in Adoption; Why Teach Art: Making Unit Studies Yours Part 2; Informal Learning; Coming Out of My Shell

Vol 6 #23: June 05: Pulling Close; Do This; Whole Grain Fiber; The Social Needs Child; Lessons from Samson & Delilah; Behind the Scenes Ministry; Bartering; Adoption: Living with "No"; Purchasing an Art Curriculum; Making Units Yours Part 3; Rewards of Volunteering

#23 June 05

Vol 6 #24: Aug 05: Boys will be Boys;

#24 Aug 05

President of the Social & Fitness Club; My Son is Learning to Cook!; Unit Yak; Online Forum; The Important; Coconut Oil; Choosing Healthy Oils; Words & Attitudes Matter; Forgiveness; Proverbs 31: The Virtuous Woman; Trust; Adoption: The Home Study; 1 Corinthians 13 for Busy Moms; Art Supplies & Materials; Making Unit Studies Yours Part 4; A Year of Cooking

#25 Oct 05

Vol 6 #25: Oct 05: Enemy at the Gate: Overseeing your Wife in Perilous Times; Raising Boys & Girls to be Grown Men & Women; Eating on the Run; Proverbs 31: Virtue; The Male Hormone Question; At-Home Mom; Adoption: The Role of Friends; Art: Age Level Criteria; All About Lap Books; Making Units Yours Part 5; Books on Tape; Unconventional College Credit; Meeting the Needs of Homeschoolers; Unit Yak; Weekly Wakeup with Kym Wright

#26 Dec 05

Vol 6 #26: Dec 05: The Worth of a Mom at Home; Christmas Traditions & Holiday Baking; Sweet Holiday Memories; Proverbs 31: An Excellent Wife; Christmas Preparation; Sharing our Failures; To The Wonderful Friends in My Circle; Seasons; Private vs Agency Adoption; Her Heart; Art: Studying from Nature; Unit Yak: Family Unity in Studies; Mini Unit: Claude Monet; Creation Science 2; Teens: Making My World a Better Place

#27 Feb 06

Vol 7 #27: Feb 06: Overseeing a Busy Mom's Life; Catching up & Cruise; Wright Photos; Soup Makes the Meal!; Proverbs 31: Spoil; SoundBites from Heaven; Self Esteem & Real Love; Adoption Promises; Weekly Wakeup: Home Atmosphere; Art: Teaching with Authority; Unit Yak: Birds; Mini Unit: van Gogh; Gift of Goals; Library Organization; Teens: Finding Your Voice

#28 April 06

Vol 7 #28: April 06: Potting Places & Lesson Plans; Unit Yak; Online Forum; Weekly Wakeup with Kym Wright: Training Up; Women: Living Life on Purpose; Bathroom Brush-Up; Easter Traditions; Purity; Pillars of Influence; Proverbs 31: She Does Him Good; Adoption Support; Special Ingredient: You; Art:

#9 Aug 98

#10 Nov 98

#11 Feb 99

#12 May 99

#13 Aug 99

Contentment; Decorating Notebook; If We Listen.

Vol 3 #9: Aug '98: A Matter of the Heart; The Harvest; Charting A Life Course; When Baby Dies in Your Womb; Recipe Experimentation; Eating Better ; Beef Dishes; Tips & Tricks; Creating Creativity; More Fun Stuff Ideas!; Once Upon A Time: Child Abuse; A Love for our Children; Trust; "Spoil"; Why are Good Books So Important; The Rest Can Wait; Women: Living Life on Purpose

Vol 3 #10: Nov '98: Children's Life Goals; The Power of the Spirit; Charting A Life Course, Pt 3; Garden of Health; Making Good Better; Faith; Growing In Grace; In Sickness or In Health; Preschool Literature; Schooling Many; One Man's Twaddle; School Organization; The Wall; Committed or Obligated? Botany; Joys of Staying Home; Ambassador of Motherhood

Vol 3 #11: Feb '99: Moving & Change; Mighty in Spirit; Adolescence; From White to Whole; Longing for an Open Womb; Adoption; Homeschooling & Organization; 'Net Connected; Correspondence College; Blessing & Dressing; Love Letter; A Journal Entry; Counting the Cost; Home & Ministry.

Vol 3 #12: May '99: Coming Home ... Again; Quiet Life; Joyful In Spirit; Children are a Blessing; Eating Better: Y2K & Beyond; Hyperchilderemia; Interstate Adoption; Raising Biological & Adopted Kids; Gentle Beauty; Preparation & Organization; Homeschooling Special Needs Children; Dean to Mom; The Professional Woman I Married; Stepping Up Your Child's Space; Scripture Memorization; A Word Kindly Spoken

Vol 4 #13: Aug '99: Standing Watch; Progress; Adolescence; Four Food Storage Plans; Menopause; Family Fitness Fun; Nausea Remedies; Healthy Granola; International Adoption; Adoption & Others; The Wait; Growing in Grace; Is the Husband Enough?; The

#14 Nov 99

#15 Feb 00

#16 May 00

#17 Aug 00

#18 Nov 00

Waltons Revisited; Classified Ads; Press On; Letting Go; A Woman of Virture; G.E.R.M. Warfare!

Vol 4 #14: Nov '99: Maintaining the Cover; "I Will"; The Father's Blessing; Is the Husband Enough? Pt 2; Grain Mills; Immuno-Woes; Teenage Birth-mothers; Wrong Reasons to Adopt; Babies Come in Many Ways; Quilting 101; Bringing Your Heart Home; Smiley Face; Older Mom; She Rises Before Dawn... to pray; Submitting; Creation Science; Good Books; Photography Unit

Vol 4 #15: Feb '00: Equipping for Excellence, Working Women, Dating/ Courtship Parameters, Settling Family Convictions, Pastry Grains, Having Healthier Children, Regaining Pre-Pregnancy Figure, Our Story of Grace (Adoption), Time Management, Homemaker or Housewife?, Learning Takes Humility, Scrapbooking, Good Books, Making Units (Studies) Yours; Scripture Memorization... Psalm 91, New Unit: Flower Arranging & Wreaths

Vol 4 #16: May '00: Discernment; Dailyness; The *Family Pow-Wow*; How Do I Get My Husband to Lead?; Grain Variety for Quick Bread; Too Tired to be Exhausted?; Getting Started in Adoption; Honoring My Husband; Finally ... Children; Moving; Titus 2:4-5— What Does It Really Mean?; Building up Child's Dreams; Homeschooling with Preschoolers; Why We Homeschool

Vol 5 #17: Aug '00: Music & Our Children; Brown Rice; Defeating Depression Naturally; Adoption Protection; Foster Parenting; Vaccinate or Not?; Stretch Travel Dollar; Unequally Yoked; LifeGuard Mom; Love Letter; Chemistry; Dissection, Autism, PDD & Celaic Disease; Recipes; Unit Study Answers from Authors

Vol 5 #18: Nov '00: Shepherding; Count Your Blessings; Basketball, Football & Music; Coaching Tight; Thanksgiving Favorites; Defeating Depression, Pt 2; Candida Yeast; Trusting the Creator; Foster Parenting; Shepherd's Crook;

#19 Feb 01

Adoption Story; Children ... a Gift; Spiritual Housecleaning; Wright Photo Gallery

Vol 5 #19: Feb '01: Serving Others; Unsaved Husbands; Whole Grain Crepes; ADD / ADHD; Bed-Wetting; Candida Questions; Weigh Down Update; Loving Baby Doe; Foster Care Resources; Tightwad Resolutions; Rising & Time with Husband: Q&A; Dream House; Special Children & Special Moms; Tag-A-Long Meals; Recipes; Baby Showers

#20 May 01

Vol 5 #20: May '01: Good-bye; An Engagement Story; Friends! Really?; Pasta Salad Italian; Cancer Prevention Tips; Cook Books; ; Keeping Our Arms Open; Becoming Your Child's Advocate; Adopting Your Foster Child; Sincerely Wondering; Frugal & Organized; Magazines; House & Garden; IEP: easy as PIE

#21 Feb 05

Vol 6 #21: Feb 05: Some Answers: A Love Letter; E-World; Catching up with the Wrights; Whole Grains: 2-Stage Process; Whole Wheat Bread; Moms Mentoring Moms; Grace in Teen Relations; Values; Empowering the Pastor's Wife; Adoption: My Spiritual Journey; Teaching Art at Home; Making Unit Studies Yours; Creation Science; Science Activities for Children; America's Junior Miss; Keepers at Home

#22 April 05

Vol 6 #22: April 05: Husband, Father, Protector: Destroyer of Lies; Purring & Italy; Dairy Dilemma; Bread-U-Cation; Awakening Love Too Soon; The Joy of Motherhood; The Expert Enabler; Finding Agreement in Adoption; Why Teach Art: Making Unit Studies Yours Part 2; Informal Learning; Coming Out of My Shell

Vol 6 #23: June 05: Pulling Close; Do This; Whole Grain Fiber; The Social Needs Child; Lessons from Samson & Delilah; Behind the Scenes Ministry; Bartering; Adoption: Living with "No"; Purchasing an Art Curriculum; Making Units Yours Part 3; Rewards of Volunteering

#23 June 05

Vol 6 #24: Aug 05: Boys will be Boys;

#24 Aug 05

President of the Social & Fitness Club; My Son is Learning to Cook!; Unit Yak; Online Forum; The Important; Coconut Oil; Choosing Healthy Oils; Words & Attitudes Matter; Forgiveness; Proverbs 31: The Virtuous Woman; Trust; Adoption: The Home Study; 1 Corinthians 13 for Busy Moms; Art Supplies & Materials; Making Unit Studies Yours Part 4; A Year of Cooking

#25 Oct 05

Vol 6 #25: Oct 05: Enemy at the Gate: Overseeing your Wife in Perilous Times; Raising Boys & Girls to be Grown Men & Women; Eating on the Run; Proverbs 31: Virtue; The Male Hormone Question; At-Home Mom; Adoption: The Role of Friends; Art: Age Level Criteria; All About Lap Books; Making Units Yours Part 5; Books on Tape; Unconventional College Credit; Meeting the Needs of Homeschoolers; Unit Yak; Weekly Wakeup with Kym Wright

#26 Dec 05

Vol 6 #26: Dec 05: The Worth of a Mom at Home; Christmas Traditions & Holiday Baking; Sweet Holiday Memories; Proverbs 31: An Excellent Wife; Christmas Preparation; Sharing our Failures; To The Wonderful Friends in My Circle; Seasons; Private vs Agency Adoption; Her Heart; Art: Studying from Nature; Unit Yak: Family Unity in Studies; Mini Unit: Claude Monet; Creation Science 2; Teens: Making My World a Better Place

#27 Feb 06

Vol 7 #27: Feb 06: Overseeing a Busy Mom's Life; Catching up & Cruise; Wright Photos; Soup Makes the Meal!; Proverbs 31: Spoil; SoundBites from Heaven; Self Esteem & Real Love; Adoption Promises; Weekly Wakeup: Home Atmosphere; Art: Teaching with Authority; Unit Yak: Birds; Mini Unit: van Gogh; Gift of Goals; Library Organization; Teens: Finding Your Voice

#28 April 06

Vol 7 #28: April 06: Potting Places & Lesson Plans; Unit Yak; Online Forum; Weekly Wakeup with Kym Wright: Training Up; Women: Living Life on Purpose; Bathroom Brush-Up; Easter Traditions; Purity; Pillars of Influence; Proverbs 31: She Does Him Good; Adoption Support; Special Ingredient: You; Art:

Learning How to Draw; Unit Yak: Turtle 101; Mini-Offices; Mini Unit: Mary Cassatt; Teens: My Top Five

Vol 7 #29: June 06: The Bread of Life; Bread Recipes; Unit Yak; Online Forum; Weekly Wakeup with Kym Wright: Comparisons; Healthy, Fun Bread Recipes; Mommy, I'm Hungry!; Let's Talk Sex!; And The Garden She Grows; Proverbs 31: Working Delighted Hands; Adoption: A Heart Like His; Before You Adopt; Art: Evaluating Student Artwork; Unit Yak: Patriotism in Art; Mini Unit: Renoir; A Framework for Family Fun; Keeping Track; Teens: Stereotypes

#29 June 06

Vol 7 #30: Aug 06: Weekly Wakeup: Do It!; When Can I Date? Proverbs 31: Merchant Ships; Adoption: Legal-Ease; Studying Art History; Unit Yak: Vote for Credit; Zoo Adventure!; Mini Unit: Carl Larsson; A Creation Science Camp; Teens: Stars in My Eyes

#30 Aug 06

Vol 7 #31: Oct 06: Mediterranean Refreshment & Cuisine; e-Couragement from Kym: Unik Yak, Weekly Wakeup, and The Mother's Journey; Women: Living Life on Purpose CD Series & Books: Children & Chores, Family Meals, Moms Mentoring Moms; Haven for the Hurting; God's Provision; Groceries the Wright Way; Sweet Smells of Autumn; Bridging the Generation Gap; Keeping First Things First; Rising Early - Another Side; Saying Goodbye to Your Wife; Studying Art History; Unit Yak: Making Units Yours: Just a Leaf; Mini Unit: Michelangelo; College: Get a Jumpstart on Life! Pageant Prep: Hair, Makeup & Tech

#31 Oct 06

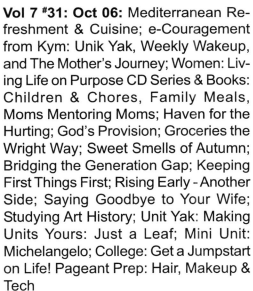

Vol 7 #32: Dec 06: The Merriest of Christmases; Wright Photos; e-Couragement from Kym: Volunteer Unit; From around the World; Kym's Talks: Moms Mentoring Moms, Family Meals, and Children & Chores; Mommy as Healthcare Giver; Finishing Strong!; A New Beginning; The Garden; A Hot Cup of Humility; Infertility: Make the Exchange; Art Journals; A Homeschool Chrismon Christmas; Obtaining Services for Special Children; Unit Yak: Making Units Yours: Introduction to Mi-

#32 Dec 06

croscopes; Microscope Adventure!; Prom Prep

Vol 8 #33: Feb 07: Burn-Out; Healthy Snacks; Preparing for Baby #8; God's Provision; Serving Our Families, Morgan's Bread Cookbook; Why Schedule? Changing Our World; Teaching Art: What to Expect of Different Age Levels; Family Garden Dreams; Garden Books & Tools, Catalogs, Month-by-Month Checklist; Homeschooling in the Maze of Autism; Mini Unit: Marc Chagall; Pageant Prep: The Box; February First Aid.

#33 Feb 07

Vol 8 #34: April 07: Whole Wheat Bread Machine Mix and Recipes; Healthy Cinnamon Buns; Simple Survival Schedule; Dana's Wise Mother; What Pastors' Wives Wish Everyone Knew; Keeping the Love in Discipline; Imaginations in My Mind; Art: Studying from Nature; Mini Unit: Paul Klee; Picturing a New Code for Spelling; Teens: My Experience in Romania; Prom Prep.

#34 April 07

Vol 8 #34: April 07: Commitment to Sisterhood; Art: Visiting a Museum; Crossfire; Library Course for Credit; Special Needs Children: Train Them Up; The Best (School) Year Ever!; The Schizophrenic Faculty; Occupying Preschoolers; What Is Giftedness?; A *Good* Government Program?; Proverbs 31: Big Cook; Pastor's Wife: Balance Life; Pageant Prep: Technical; Punching the Clock: Time Management for Moms?; Time: An Irreplaceable Commodity; Milled Flour from Whole Grains

#34 April 07

Hands-on Unit Studies from
Learn and Do

Microscope Adventure!

With hints on buying a microscope to how to use it effectively, this unit covers it all! The $1 Rule of Optics, people to study, how to make permanent, semipermanent, well, wet and dry mounts. With the lab sheets included, use inexpensive items around the house, to study plant & animal cells, microbes, fibers, insects, crystals and more. Draw observations and fill in scientific data on lab sheets. 4th grade & up.

Photography Unit

Learn camera parts & types, along with up-to-date information on digital cameras. Understand lenses & film, composing pictures, focal point, lighting & angles. Practice photographing people, silhouettes, groups, portraits & children. Landscape, panorama, action shots, photographing animals, special effects & more. 4th grade & up.

Botany Unit

One of the best sellers in our catalog of studies. Learn all about plants from the roots up. Life cycles, needs, usage, differences, uniqueness, and comparisons. Microscopic to hands-on labs with plenty of Lab Sheets and flashcards provided. Appropriate for 6th grade through high school ~ this 160+ page study provides an exciting and comprehensive look at the plant world around us.

COLOR! Unit

with an interactive CD!: a terrific hands-on experience for learning color theory and its applications in fine art. This very interesting & entertaining unit will expose your students to color through exploration of fine art reproductions, the theory behind why certain color combinations work together and others don't. Full-color examples & hands-on labs, sure to capture the imagination of even the most kinesthetic student.

Library Unit

How to use the library, obtain a card, know the rules, learn etiquette and how the library is organized. Create personal reading lists, library notebook & library bag - all to save time at the library & improve our skills. Go online to look up books, reserve resources, and access interlibrary loans. Build a library, start a story hour, memorize the Dewey Decimal System, & earn high school credit for the course. 3rd & up

Bird Unit Study

Dubbed "Unit Studies for the Clueless" by Mary Pride's reviewer, it includes everything needed for a comprehensive study of birds. With lots of hands-on activities, it's a "no-brainer" - for mom/teacher, anyway. Sit back and learn along with the students. Identify birds in the field, air, or on water. Research projects help you learn bird species, beaks, feet, habitat, and incubating eggs.

Turtles! Unit

with a phenomenal CD of an actual dissection!: We all love turtles - watching & feeding them. Dig deeper and learn turtle anatomy along with the difference between reptiles and amphibians. Can you tell a turtle's age by its shell? How long do they live? Dissection included, to see the fascinating way turtles are created. Learn how to open the shell and all the external and internal parts. Since there was so much information for the required FunSheets™, we split it into two age levels: Younger (Pre-K-4th) and Older (4th-adult). While they both include some pages the same (Turtle Report, Plant or Animal, Anatomy, Sea Turtles), the presentation is different.

Younger Turtle FunSheets™: a must-have to go with the Turtles! Unit, for ages pre-K-4th. Includes graphs, mapwork, 3 turtle diet booklets, turtle identification with stickers, turtle vs tortoise worksheets, life cycles, and sea turtles graphs.

Older Turtle FunSheets™: includes observation graphs, mapwork, chordates research, measuring turtles, complete dissection, turtle vs tortoise research, various names for turtles, taxonomical classification, dietary preferences charts and sea turtles research.

Hands-on Unit Studies from
Learn and Do

Spiders Unit

90-pages & gives a solid foundation in spiders, systematically studying: taxonomy, internal and external anatomy, diet, life cycle, habits, habitats, venomous types, handling, observations, experiments, webs, silk, and more.

Victorian Sewing and Quilting

Learn to quilt, bead, make sachets and Victorian pillows. Study color, harmonies, and the color wheel's application to fabric. Sew with modern and antique lace. Especially appropriate for the aspiring homemaker ~ appropriate for 6th grade through adult.

Flower Arranging and Wreaths

Study the wonderful art of floral arrangement and crafts, along with making wreaths, all in a systematic approach. Colleges teach this type course as "Horticulture 352: Flower Arranging." Enough for a one-semester high school credit. With marketing plans & practice, it becomes a one-year high school credit.

Goat Unit

70+ pages of fun, learning and hands-on activities. Practice milking at home without a goat! Anatomy, genetics and practical raisin' requirements are discussed, researched and practiced. This study is a guide to assist you in getting to know goat breeds and needs. A marketing and business plan is also included. All ages.

Sheep Unit

covers literature, history, hands-on fun, practical how-to's, raisin' requirements, anatomy, shearing, washing fleece and craft ideas. Learn the breeds, needs and feeds of sheep. Learning and fun for the whole family. All ages.

Poultry Unit

covers chickens, ducks, turkeys, and geese. Learn about incubating, raising and breeding. Supermarket Dissection, Lab Sheets, and plenty of Fun SheetsTM are included. All ages.

Arachnid Unit

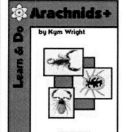

covers the study of scorpions, pseudo-scorpions, whip scorpions, mini whip scorpions, mites, ticks, harvestmen and others. Makes a great companion study to the Spiders Unit. Study arachnids, their taxonomy, size, habits and habitats. Activities, labs, questions and information help you discover all about harvestmen, mites, chiggers, and ticks as well! So, come along on an Arachnid Adventure!

Volunteer Unit

As our homeschool children turn into preteens and teens, we see a need to help them learn about the world in preparation for their upcoming lives as adults: hands-on experiences, to see the poverty, the need, and take part in bringing hope and healing. Working with established groups, creating your own, or volunteering individually, there are always opportunities for service. 4th grade & up.

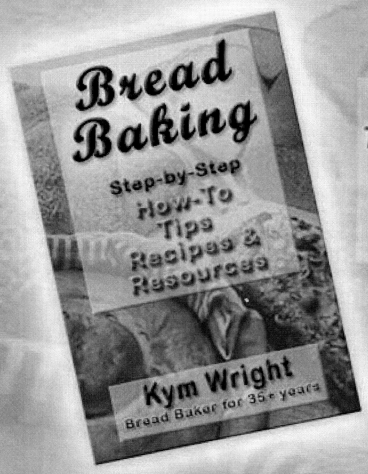

Free e-Couragement™
from Kym

Get your weekly dose of free encouragement from Kym Wright!

An invitation from Kym:

One of my favorite verses about motherhood is when Deborah, a judge of Israel, and a woman of might in battle, sings a song to the Lord,

Until I, Deborah, arose, until I arose, a mother in Israel. Judges 5:7 b, c

That's my prayer for us, that we arise to become the moms God has intended for us to be. It won't look the same in each family, but it will be based on a similar foundation of love, respect, time, training, discipline, discipling, fun, encouragement and all of those other aspects we admire and need.

Join us?

From one mother to another,

Kym Wright

Welcome to the **Unit Yak!** a **free monthly e-zine** for unit study users – and those who are interested.

E-zine, E-Couragement, E-xactly!

The basic concept of unit studies is using one topic or literary selection to incorporate the majority of school subjects, especially: science, history,

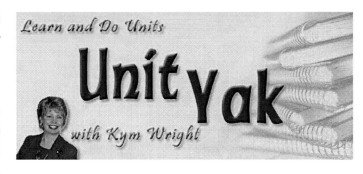

social studies and geography, writing, art and reading. Most times, math and grammar concepts are studied separately from the unit, but can be practiced within its context. There are primarily three ways to obtain unit studies:

- use what is available on the market
- heavily customize one that you find
- write your own

Kym shares a practical approach to schooling using unit studies, along with tips on how to make it work for you, your students, and your homeschool. Join Kym as she gives advice, and shares hints which make unit studies come alive. From the planning, gathering materials and supplies, record-keeping and actually teaching - Kym helps and encourages you along the way.

Living Life on Purpose

Qty	Women: Living Life on Purpose	Print	eBook	Info	Total
	Living Life on Purpose 3rd Edition	$19.95	N/A	Info	$

CD Sets & Books

	Magazine Article Writing 6 CD Set	$39.95	N/A	Info	$
	Family Meals 3 CD & Book Set	$19.95	N/A	Info	$
	Children & Chores 3 CD & Book Set	$19.95	N/A	Info	$
	Creating Creativity CD	$8.95	N/A	Info	$
	Moms Mentoring Moms CD	$8.95	N/A	Info	$
	Gift of Goals CD	$8.95	N/A	Info	$

Living Life on Purpose Total: $

The Mother's Heart Magazine
(formerly *Open Arms Magazine*)

Qty	Description	Print	eBook	Info	Total
	1 Year e-Subscription (6 Issues)	N/A	$21.95	Info	$
	2 Year e-Subscription (12 Issues)	N/A	$39.95	Info	$
	Back Issues (eBook)	N/A	$4.00	Info	$
	Yearly Anthology (eBook) Check one	N/A	$21.95	Info	$
	☐#1 ☐#2 ☐#3 ☐#4 ☐#5 ☐#6 ☐#7				

The Mother's Heart Total: $

Make Check Payable to:
alWright Publishing
PO Box 81124
Conyers, GA 30013
Postage included in price.
US Funds, please.

Unit Studies Total: $
TMH Magazine Total: $
Living Life on Purpose Total: $

Total Order: $

Learn and Do Unit Studies

Qty	Description	Print	eBook	Info	Total
	Arachnids Unit Study	$17.95	$15.95	Info	$
	Bird Unit Study	$17.95	$15.95	Info	$
	Botany Unit Study	$21.95	$19.95	Info	$
	Extra Botany Flash Cards	$8.00	N/A	Info	$
	Extra Botany Lab Sheets	$8.00	N/A	Info	$
	Bread Baking Unit Study	N/A	$9.95	Info	
	Color Unit Study w/CD	$17.95	$15.95	Info	$
	Flower Arranging & Wreaths	$14.95	$12.95	Info	$
	Goat Unit Study	$13.95	$11.95	Info	$
	Library Unit Study	$19.95	$17.95	Info	$
	Microscope Adventure!	$17.95	$15.95	Info	$
	Extra Microscope Lab Sheets	$8.00	N/A	Info	$
	Photography Unit Study	$15.95	$13.95	Info	$
	Poultry Unit Study	$15.95	$13.95	Info	$
	Sheep Unit Study	$13.95	$11.95	Info	$
	Spider Unit Study	$17.95	$15.95	Info	$
	Turtles Unit Study w/CD	$15.95	$23.95	Info	$
	Turtles Activity Pack - Older	$8.00	included	Info	$
	Turtles Activity Pack - Younger	$8.00	included	Info	$
	Victorian Sewing	$15.95	$13.95	Info	$
	Volunteer Unit Study	$19.95	$17.95	Info	$
	Organizing the Queen (Pageant help)	$7.95	$7.95	Info	$

Unit Studies Total $